Democracy and Enlargement in Post-Communist Europe

Democracy and Enlargement in Post-Communist Europe presents the principal findings of a unique in-depth study of the birth of democracy and the market economy in fifteen post-Communist countries. Haerpfer analyses and compares the quantitative information collected by the New Democracies Barometer public opinion surveys to provide an overview of the process of democratisation across Central and Eastern Europe.

The book investigates what the general public thought of a wide range of issues including:

- European identity of post-Communist citizens
- the European Union – enlargement and integration
- Communism and other non-democratic regimes
- military integration into NATO and international security issues
- birth of democracy
- birth of the market economy

This is an extremely valuable resource and will be useful for all those interested in the European Union, European identity, comparative politics, democracy and the Communist legacy. It contains comparative and empirical data from Belarus, Bulgaria, Croatia, the Czech Republic, Estonia, the Federal Republic of Yugoslavia, Hungary, Latvia, Lithuania, Poland, Romania, the Russian Federation, Slovakia, Slovenia and the Ukraine.

Christian W. Haerpfer is Director of the Centre for Strategic Development at the Institute for Advanced Studies, Vienna and teaches Political Science at the University of Vienna. He is an academic consultant for the European Commission, the British Government and for the Romanian Federal Government in Central and Eastern European affairs.

Routledge Advances in European Politics

Democracy and Enlargement in Post-Communist Europe

The democratisation of the general public in fifteen Central and Eastern European countries, 1991–1998

Christian W. Haerpfer

London and New York

To Harry, my faithful companion in a period of change

First published 2002
by Routledge
11 New Fetter Lane, London EC4P 4EE

Simultaneously published in the USA and Canada
by Routledge
29 West 35th Street, New York, NY 10001

Routledge is an imprint of the Taylor & Francis Group

Typeset in 10/12 Baskerville by Wearset Ltd, Boldon, Tyne and Wear
Printed and bound in Great Britain by Biddles Ltd, Guildford and
King's Lynn

British Library Cataloguing in Publication Data
A catalogue record for this book is available from the British Library

Library of Congress Cataloging in Publication Data
Haerpfer, Christian W.
 Democracy and enlargement in post-Communist Europe : the
democratisation of the general public in fifteen Central and Eastern
European countries, 1991–1998 / Christian W. Haerpfer.
 p. cm.
 Simultaneously pubished in the USA and Canada.
 1. Democracy–Europe, Eastern–Public opinion. Includes
bibliographical references and index. 2. Democratisation–Europe,
Eastern–Public opinion. 3. Europe–Economic integration–Public
opinion. 4. Public opinion–Europe, Eastern. I. Title.

JN96.A58 H34 2002
320.947–dc21
                                        2002069874

ISBN 0–415–27422–2

Contents

Tables

Preface and acknowledgements

This book is the outcome of a decade of cross-national and empirical research on political transformations in post-Communist Europe since 1990. In 1990, I decided to analyse the processes of democratisation and marketisation in Central and Eastern Europe with a large-scale research programme, the 'New Democracies Barometer'. This book compiles in a systematic way the results of all five waves of the New Democracies Barometer between 1991 and 1998 and attempts to offer a distinct theoretical approach to the analysis of democratisation in post-Communist Europe. This research, which is the empirical basis of the book, was planned and discussed by Richard Rose, the international scientific adviser of the New Democracies Barometer and the author at conferences, seminars, lunches and dinners in Washington, New York, Boston, New Haven, London, Colchester, Glasgow, Helensburgh, Brussels, Berlin, Florence, Warsaw, Prague and Vienna. This book would have been impossible without the energy, foresight and creativity of Richard Rose, with whom the author has written more than fifty publications about the political and economic transformations after 1989.

The New Democracies Barometer was a very long and expensive research programme, involving more than 60,000 face-to-face interviews in twelve post-Communist countries. This ambitious research programme was made possible by generous financial support from the Austrian National Bank and the Austrian Ministry of Science and Research. At the Austrian National Bank, the continued support of President Adolf Wala, President Maria Schaumayr and Governor Liebscher is gratefully acknowledged. Within the Austrian Ministry of Science and Research, special thanks go to Minister Erhard Busek and Minister Rudolf Scholten and especially to Sektionschef Norbert Rozsenich, who never faltered in his help to keep the New Democracies Barometer going. At the Ministry of Science and Research, Andrea Schmölzer and Günther Burkhart were always excellent partners in planning, implementing and presenting the five waves of this successful research programme in the social sciences. The organisational basis of the New Democracies Barometer between 1991 and 1998 was the Paul Lazarsfeld Society, where I had the honour to serve as scientific director at that time. The driving force in that scientific society and behind the New Democracies Barometer was Heinz Kienzl, who was responsible for the financial and organisational basis of the New Democracies Barometer. His help and support through all these years was particularly important for the success of this Austrian research pro-gramme in the social and political sciences. His energy and negotiation skills with the Ministry of Science and Research and the Austrian National Bank were the necessary preconditions for the creation and continuity of the New Democracies Barometer

After the end of the complex and long fieldwork in five consecutive waves between 1991 and 1998 in twelve European countries, the writing of the book took place between 1999 and 2001 and coincided with my won-derful intellectual and personal partnership with Claire Wallace from the Institute for Advanced Studies in Vienna. She persuaded me to write this book and her support, understanding and patience were crucial for the finalisation of the manuscript. We discussed this book in Moscow, Kiev, Yalta, Minsk, Sofia, Bucharest, Budapest, Prague, Dartmoor, London, Derby, Vienna and – many times – in Klosterneuburg in the Vienna woods.

I would like to thank Stephen White from Glasgow University, Hans-Dieter Klingemann from the Science Centre, Berlin, Juan Linz from Yale University, Eva Kreisky, Hans-Georg Heinrich, Peter Gerlich, Helmut Kramer, Peter Ulram, Thomas Nowotny, all at the University of Vienna, Fritz Plasser, Innsbruck University, for their professional and intellectual support over the years and their trust that my New Democracies Barometer is a worthwhile academic venture in comparative politics.

First drafts of Chapter 7 were written at the University of Essex during an ECASS Fellowship in summer 1997. The support of Jay Gershunny, Marcia Taylor, John Brice and Kate Tucker at the University of Essex is gratefully acknowledged. The first draft of Chapter 1 was written during a very pleasant EUSSIRF Fellowship at the Robert Schuman Centre at the European University Institute in Florence in summer 1999. The friendly support of Jan Zielonka, Patricia Fregosi and Peter Kennealy formed – together with Florence in particular and Tuscany in general – an enjoy-able environment. The Fellowships in Colchester and Florence were funded by the European Commission, Directorate General Research. Parts of the research work, communication with scholars in comparative politics all over Europe and the writing in 2000 and 2001 were supported by the European Science Foundation within the framework of the ESF Network 'Citizens in Transition'. The secretary for the Social Sciences at the European Science Foundation at the time, John Smith, was particu-larly helpful in launching this European network of scholars in compara-tive politics.

I learned a lot from my colleagues in Central and Eastern Europe, with whom I collaborated in many ways and in many places between January

1990 and the end of the century: Zdenka Mansfeldova (Czech Academy of Sciences, Prague), Ladislav Machacek (Slovak Academy of Sciences, Bratislava), Wladislaw Adamski (Polish Academy of Sciences, Warsaw), Sijka Kovatcheva (University of Plovdiv, Bulgaria), Dorel Abraham (Institute for Urban and Regional Studies, Bucharest), David Rotman (University of Minsk, Belarus), Sergei Tumanov (Moscow State University) and Valeri Nikolejevski (University of Kharkiv, the Ukraine).

I would also like to thank Bernhard Felderer, Christian Helmenstein, and Veronika Turek from the Institute for Advanced Studies in Vienna for the invitation to work in this prestigious research Institute as Director of the Centre for Strategic Development; the pleasant atmosphere provided the right environment and the adequate resources for writing this book.

I am grateful to all of them for their time, their ideas, insights, support and friendship. None of the above scholars and personalities is responsible for this book and its content; the responsibility is entirely mine.

This book was made possible by the personal, emotional and intellectual support of my whole family, especially Claire Wallace, Bärbl Weinzierl, Bruno Weinzierl and my mother, Christl Haerpfer. The book is dedicated in love and friendship to my late friend Harry, who listened faithfully and loyally to my monologues about the emerging book during long and wonderful walks with him in the Vienna woods.

1 The concept of democratisation and democracy

The process of democratisation, which took place after 1989 in post-Communist Europe, is part of the 'third wave of democratisation' according to the terminology of Samuel Huntington (1991). This third wave of democratisation started in 1974 and took place in Portugal, Spain and somewhat later in Central and Eastern Europe, after the *annus mirabilis* of autumn 1989.

The literature on democratisation in general distinguishes between three different theoretical approaches (Potter *et al.* 1997): Potter *et al.* label these three approaches the 'modernization approach', the 'transition approach', and the 'structural approach'. The theoretical ambition of this book consists of proposing a fourth approach to analyse the processes of democratisation, a theoretical concept, which I call the 'transformation approach'. The 'modernization approach' is closely linked to the work of Seymour Martin Lipset during the 1960s and 1970s and is represented in the 1980s and 1990s in a very prolific way by Larry Diamond (1999). The 'transition approach' was developed primarily by Dankwart Rostow and is now presented very prominently by Guillermo O'Donnell and especially by Juan Linz and Alfred Stepan (Linz and Stepan 1996). The structural approach was put forward primarily by Anthony Giddens (Giddens 1993), Barrington Moore in the 1960s (Moore 1966) and by Dietrich Rueschemeyer in the 1990s (Rueschemeyer, *et al.* 1992).

Three central processes

The 'transformation approach', which is presented for the first time in this book, can be characterised by three central processes:

Process 1: democratisation towards democracy.
Process 2: marketisation towards market economy.
Process 3: creation of civil society.

The specific characteristics of the post-Communist transition consist in the fact that we are witnessing not only a political transformation from a totalitarian regime to a pluralistic democracy, but at the same time an economic transformation from a planned command economy to a free market economy in Central and Eastern Europe and finally a transformation towards a civil society with free associations. One of the deepest and most dramatic as well as most visible structural changes after 1989 consisted in the transformation from a centrally planned economy to a decentralised market economy in a very short period, the creation of entirely new economic actors and the building of new economic institutions and a legal framework to ensure the freedom of economic activity. Whereas there had been historical examples of successful processes of democratisation, for example, in Greece, Spain and Portugal – to name a few members of the European Union, which have successfully managed the difficult transition from authoritarian rule towards democracy – Europe had no experience of transforming a planned economy into a market economy. Hence, the economic transformation after 1989 in Central and Eastern Europe was possibly even more difficult and cumbersome than the political transformation from a totalitarian regime to a pluralistic democracy.

This book deals only with the first process of democratisation, not with the other essential processes of marketisation nor with the building up of social capital in an emerging civil society. These other important transformation processes will be analysed in forthcoming publications. The transformation approach and its dimensions can be shown in Table 1.1.

This book deals only with field 4, the behaviour and attitudes of post-Communist citizens in the new political regimes and their relationship to democracy. The transformation approach also encompasses five other fields, on the macro-level the new political systems and the new economic systems as well as the variety of associations and NGOs as part of the emerging civil society. At the micro-level, the transformation approach also analyses the economic behaviour of post-Communist households and the formation of social capital at the level of the individual. In order to develop a theory of post-Communist transformation, one has to take into

Table 1.1 The transformation approach

Transformation process		
Democracy	Market economy	Civil society
Democratisation	Marketisation	Creation of social capital
Macro-level		
Political system and institutions (1)	Economic system and institutions (2)	Social associations (3)
Micro-level		
Citizens (4)	Households (5), companies	Social capital (6)

account all six fields of research. Hence, this book is only the very first step in the explanation of political transformations since 1989 in post-Communist Europe.

Democratisation as an open-ended process

A core conceptual assumption of the transformation approach is that we should not speak of 'transition', but of 'transformation'. The term transition implies that there is a passage from a state A to a certain state B, from a Communist political system towards liberal democracy, from a centrally planned economy to a market economy. The concept of transition suggests a clear end-point of political development, for example, a pluralist and liberal democracy, for theoreticians of transition the process of change is a clear track from point A to point B, transition theory defines the goal of change and deciding when this goal is reached and transition completed. At the level of the political system, we see state A, e.g. a Communist party system, a transition period away from state A and the arrival at state B, a liberal democracy. This static approach is not used by the transformation approach, which regards the variety of political changes after 1989 as dynamic and open. The transformation approach does not postulate a 'quasi-natural' aim and goal of changes, the outcome of political as well as economic transformations is open and not given at the beginning or during the comparative analysis of change.

Cross-national comparison

The comparative method used is not a case study of one or a few countries, but a systematic comparison of a variety of countries. The transformation approach, as represented in this book, is not aiming at this stage at universal, worldwide explications. The concepts used in that approach are valid only for those European countries, which were liberated from Communism after 1989. These countries we label as 'post-Communist', the universe of my transformation approach is currently restricted to the following 'transformation countries':

1   Central Europe: the Czech Republic (1), Hungary (2), Poland (3), Slovakia (4), Slovenia (5).
2   Southern Europe: Bulgaria (6), Croatia (7), the Federal Republic of Yugoslavia (8), Romania (9).
3   Northern Europe: Estonia (10), Latvia (11), Lithuania (12).
4   Eastern Europe: Belarus (13), the Russian Federation (14), the Ukraine (15).

These fifteen post-Communist countries form the geographical region covered by this book. Other countries are also part of the 'universe' of the transformation approach, but are not analysed here and they will be the subjects of forthcoming transformation studies: Albania, Macedonia, Moldova, Armenia, Georgia and Kyrgystan, Kazakhstan.

Comparison over time during transformation

Beyond the cross-national comparison the longitudinal comparison over time is the second form of comparison used by the transformation approach. It is important to measure the different stages of trans- formation repeatedly in order to monitor the processes of changes, while they are happening, not afterwards. The data points of measurement con- cerning the process of democratisation in this book are 1991, 1992, 1994, 1996 and 1998. The cross-national comparison of fifteen post-Communist nations and the over-time comparison of five data points between 1991 and 1998 result in a complex country–time matrix as the central basis for empirical evidence to ground the theoretical approach.

The database of the book

A longitudinal large-scale and cross-national survey, the New Democracies Barometer, on economic and political changes in Central and Eastern Europe has been conducted by the author with an average of 10,000 interviews per year since 1991. The first and foremost aim of that bi-annual survey is the regular monitoring of general public reactions in post-Communist Central and Eastern Europe to the economic, social and political transformations since the demise of Communism and the subject- ive quality of life, especially the standard of living of post-Communist cit- izens. The following countries are covered in this longitudinal study, as shown in Table 1.2.

Table 1.2 New Democracies Barometer: countries and points of measurement

Country	NDB 1	NDB 2	NDB 3	NDB 4	NDB 5
Belarus	*	1992	1994	1996	1998
Bulgaria	1991	1992	1994	1996	1998
Czech Republic	1991	1992	1994	1996	1998
Croatia	*	1992	1994	1996	1998
FR of Yugoslavia	*	*	*	*	1998
Hungary	1991	1992	1994	1996	1998
Poland	1991	1992	1994	1996	1998
Romania	1991	1992	1994	1996	1998
Russia	*	*	1994	*	*
Slovakia	1991	1992	1994	1996	1998
Slovenia	1991	1992	1994	1996	1998
Ukraine	*	1992	1994	1996	1998

Note: * Not done in this country at this time.

The countries and points of measurement for the New Baltics Barometer (NBB) are shown.

1	Estonia	NBB	1995	1996
2	Lithuania	NBB	1995	1996
3	Latvia	NBB	1995	1996

My cross-national survey is called the New Democracies Barometer (= NDB) and was conducted in 1991 (= New Democracies Barometer I), in 1992 (= New Democracies Barometer II), in 1994 (= New Democracies Barometer III), in 1996 (= New Democracies Barometer IV). The last round of that longitudinal Ten-Nation Study took place in February–March 1998 (= New Democracies Barometer V).

The fieldwork of the New Democracies Barometer has been subcontracted to national partners in the twelve countries. All twelve national partners have to fulfil the so-called ESOMAR standards and are either academic institutes in the social sciences or commercial private enterprises. In each of the twelve countries, around 1,000 respondents were surveyed in face-to-face interviews (for details see the Appendix). The basic sampling procedure in each country follows ESOMAR principles of a multi-stage, random probability sample, in which the population is stratified regionally and within regions according to urban–rural divisions and town size. One hundred or more primary sampling units (PSU) were drawn in each country. Within each PSU individual respondents were chosen on the basis of standard random procedures, such as the Kish matrix or selecting the household member next having a birthday.

2 Nostalgia for the Communist past and support for the restoration of Communism

Assessment of the micro-economic standard of living of their own household under Communism

The first section of this chapter deals with the assessment of the economic situation of the household before 1989. Which post-Communist households were in a better economic situation in a system of centrally planned economies? One central outcome of this analysis consists in the fact that the majority of all post-Communist households were in a better financial and economic situation before the Revolution of 1989, when they are asked to compare their actual economic situation with the situation before 1989. In 1991, 63 per cent of all post-Communist households in all ten countries indicated that the economic situation of their own household was much better or a little better under the *ancien régime* (see Table 2.1). This share of households with a deteriorating financial standard of living increased until 1994 even to 66 per cent of all households between Prague and Kiev. Between 1994 and 1998, the percentage of losing households went down again to 63 per cent of all households. The longitudinal patterns are very different in Central Europe as compared with South-East Europe: at the beginning of the economic transformation in 1991, 66 per cent of all Central European households were better off before 1989, but that share melted down in a slow and linear way during the first phase of transition to 55 per cent in 1998. The development in South-East Europe was exactly the opposite: in 1991, 57 per cent of the post-Communist households in that region indicated that they had been better off before the transformation started, but the share of households which were better off before 1989 increased up to 72 per cent of all households in Southern and Eastern Europe. In the course of the first nine years of economic transformation, the households in South-East Europe look at their standard of living under Communism in a much more favourable perspective than the households in Central Europe.

The Central European economy with the greatest share of households, which had a better financial standard of living under Communism, is the Hungarian economy of the 1980s. In 1991, 68 per cent of all Hungarian

Table 2.1 Households which were economically better off before 1989

Q. When you compare the overall economic situation of your household before the big changes in the economy in 1989, would you say that in the past it was much better or a little better? (Percentage of households which had a much better and a little better economic situation *before* 1989)

Country	NDB 1 1991	NDB 2 1992	NDB 3 1994	NDB 4 1996	NDB 5 1998	Change 1991–8
Central Europe	66	63	61	53	55	−11
Hungary	68	73	75	72	72	4
Slovakia	68	62	63	59	54	−14
Poland	61	68	62	50	51	−10
Slovenia	80	62	53	45	50	−30
Czech Republic	53	51	50	39	46	−7
Southern Europe	57	54	62	65	63	12
FR of Yugoslavia	*	*	*	*	86	*
Croatia	*	*	70	70	70	0
Bulgaria	66	54	59	59	60	−6
Romania	47	53	56	66	59	12
Northern Europe	*	*	63	58	*	−5
Latvia	*	*	68	69	*	1
Lithuania	*	*	69	62	*	−7
Estonia	*	*	53	43	*	−10
Eastern Europe	*	76	85	80	85	9
Ukraine	*	80	88	78	90	10
Belarus	*	71	82	82	79	8
Russia	*	*	65	*	*	*

Note
* Not done in this country at this time.

households said that their standard of living was higher before 1989. That percentage even went up to 75 per cent in 1994, but is now, in the second half of the 1990s, at the level of 72 per cent of all Hungarian households, which is by far the highest compared to the other candidates for the enlargement of the European Union. In Slovakia, the share of households with a decreasing standard of living was, with 68 per cent, as high as in Hungary, but the numbers of Slovakian households which had been better off before 1989 shrank during the process of micro-economic trans-formation in a linear and steady development to 54 per cent in 1998. In Poland, the share of losing households went steeply up from 61 per cent in 1991 to 68 per cent in 1992, but shrank since 1992 down to 51 per cent of all Polish households in 1998. The changes at the level of households in Central Europe were most dramatic in Slovenia, where 80 per cent of all Slovenian households declared in 1991 that they are now worse off com-pared with their micro-economic situation in former Yugoslavia. This enormous share of losing Slovenian households decreased steadily to 50 per cent in 1998. The Czech Republic had the best starting position: only 53 per cent of all Czech households had a lower economic standard of living in 1991, if compared with their experience under Czech Communism. That percentage went down to 39 per cent in 1996, but increased again during the recent Czech economic crisis in 1998 to 46 per cent. If one is discussing the comparative assessment of the micro-economic past under Communism with the micro-economic present during the process of economic transformation in Central Europe, one should bear in mind that even after nine years of transition, we can still identify between 46 and 72 per cent of all Central European post-Communist households, which have the subjective impression that the financial–economic situation of their own household was better under Communism in comparison with the actual transition economy.

In Southern and Eastern Europe, the number of households which had a better standard of living under Communism is much higher in comparison with the micro-economic conditions in the Central European buffer zone. The economy with the strongest financial deterioration of individual households in Eastern Europe is the Ukraine: at the beginning of economic transformation in 1992, 80 per cent of all Ukrainian households indicated that their standard of living was better in the Soviet Union. During the first stage of economic transition, this extremely high share of losing households went up further to 90 per cent in 1998, who perceived their current standard of living as worse than ten years ago. In the Federal Republic of Yugoslavia, 86 per cent of all households in Serbia and Montenegro declared in 1998 that they had a better micro-economic situation in the former Yugoslavia before 1989. A similar pattern at a slightly lower level than in the Ukraine we find in Belarus: at the beginning of economic transition in 1992, 71 per cent of all Byelorussian households have the subjective perception that their economic situation was much better or somewhat better in the former Soviet Union. That share of losing households in Belarus increased to 82 per cent in 1994 and went down a little to 79 per cent in 1998.

We did not find any longitudinal pattern in the Croatian transition economy: a constant share of 70 per cent of all Croatian households declared between 1994 and 1998 that their financial standard of living was better before the economic revolution after 1989. In the Russian Federation, 65 per cent of all Russian households had a better economic situation in the period of the Soviet Union, compared with 1994 at the beginning of post-Communist economic transformation. The pattern over time in Bulgaria and Romania shows a clear-cut convergence: the share of losing households went down from 66 per cent in 1991 to 60 per cent in 1998, whereas the Romanian households started in a more favourable position with a share of 47 per cent of losing households in 1991, but approaching the Bulgarian level with 59 per cent of all Romanian households, who stated in 1998 that they had been better off under Communism.

Nostalgia for the previous Communist economic system

Concerning the old economic system, we can quantify the extent of support for the former centralised and bureaucratic planned economy, which had operated in most of the analysed countries for forty or more years, before it collapsed very quickly in 1989 (see Table 2.2). The indicator of satisfaction with the planned economy before 1989 gives the command economy a rating between +10 and +100, where +100 is very positive and +10 somewhat positive.

The overall picture concerning the past economic system for all nine countries is one of increasing nostalgia for the economic stability of the past, when compared with the speed of economic changes and economic instability since 1989. In 1991, 51 per cent of all Central and East European citizens had a positive assessment of the old economic system. That share of persons with preference for the previous economic system went up to 58 per cent in 1992 and reached its peak in 1994, when 62 per cent of all post-Communist citizens displayed positive attitudes towards the planned economy before 1989. The nostalgia for the macro-economic

Table 2.2 Nostalgia for the former Communist economic system

Q. Here is a scale for ranking how the economy works. The top, +100, is the best; at the bottom, −100, is the worst. Where on this scale would you put the socialist economy?

Country	NDB 1 1991	NDB 2 1992	NDB 3 1994	NDB 4 1996	NDB 5 1998	Change 1991–8
Central Europe	51	56	58	53	55	4
Hungary	69	74	75	69	70	1
Slovakia	61	61	74	71	64	3
Slovenia	42	46	48	47	55	13
Czech Republic	42	44	42	40	47	5
Poland	43	57	52	38	41	−2
Southern Europe						
FR of Yugoslavia	*	*	*	*	79	*
Bulgaria	48	59	66	75	58	10
Croatia	*	28	44	40	53	25
Romania	50	57	60	50	45	−5
Northern Europe	*	*	73	72	*	−1
Latvia	*	*	68	79	*	11
Lithuania	*	*	81	77	*	−4
Estonia	*	*	71	61	*	−10
Eastern Europe	*	76	77	89	84	8
Ukraine	*	76	76	90	90	14
Belarus	*	76	78	88	78	2
Russia	*	*	61	*	*	*

Notes
* Not done in this country at this time.
People with positive attitudes: +10 to +100.

past went down from 61 per cent in 1996 to 54 per cent of all respondents in all nine countries in 1998. We can therefore speak of a decline of economic nostalgia in Central and Eastern Europe since 1996.

The nostalgia for the Communist economy was lowest between 1991 and 1996 in the Czech Republic with a share of 40 per cent of the Czech population expressing some sympathy for the Czech planned economy. The recent economic turbulences in the Czech Republic resulted in the fact that the percentage of Czechs who have a positive assessment of the past economic regime went up from 40 per cent in 1996 to 47 per cent of the Czech population in 1998 (Haerpfer and Wallace 1998). Poland displayed an entirely different pattern: the nostalgia for the planned economy was highest in 1992 with 57 per cent of the Polish population having positive evaluations of the Communist economy, but this group shrank in size during the 1990s after the 'big bang' economic reforms of the Polish economy in the early 1990s. In spring 1998, only 41 per cent of the Polish population had positive attitudes towards the past economic system, the lowest value compared with all other Central and Eastern economies analysed in the report.

The support for the planned economy in Romania has the following pattern: in 1991, 50 per cent of the Romanian population thought in a somewhat positive way about the Communist economic regime before 1989; that went up in the early 1990s to a peak of 60 per cent, but since 1994 the share of nostalgic Romanians had decreased to 50 per cent in 1996 and finally to 45 per cent in 1998. The longitudinal pattern in Croatia is again very different: in 1992, when the euphoria about the new established state of Croatia overshadowed almost all other considerations and attitudes, only 28 per cent of the Croatian population expressed positive feelings towards the Yugoslav economy of the past. That small share of Croatian nostalgic citizens grew to 44 per cent in 1994 and reached a peak in spring 1998 with 53 per cent. The national pride in the early 1990s was replaced by growing disillusionment with the war economy and subsequent nostalgia for the relatively prosperous economy of former Yugoslavia.

A similar pattern could be found in Slovenia, where 42 per cent expressed some nostalgia about the Yugoslav economy in 1991, a figure that increased steadily to 55 per cent in 1998. If one analyses Slovenia, Croatia and the Federal Republic of Yugoslavia (= Serbia plus Montenegro) together, the most prominent feature consists of a strong nostalgia for the economic system of former Yugoslavia. In terms of satisfaction with the general economic system, we can speak of a clear and strong dissatisfaction of all previous member states of Yugoslavia with the current economy. The slow transformation of the Bulgarian economy between 1991 and 1996 resulted in a steady increase of the share of Bulgarian population, who were nostalgic about the previous economic system from 48 per cent in 1991 up to 75 per cent in 1996. The level of macro-economic dissatisfaction in 1996 was similar to the constant and massive economic discontent with the emerging market economy in countries like the Ukraine or Belarus during the 1990s. Between 1996 and 1998, the percentage of nostalgic Bulgarians decreased from the peak value of 75 per cent to 58 per cent, which indicates less nostalgia for the old economic system and growing satisfaction with the emerging market economy. The nostalgia for the Czechoslovak economy in Slovakia was much higher than in the Czech Republic. The peak of Slovak nostalgia for the previous economic system took place in 1994, when 74 per cent of the Slovakian population thought positively about the former Czechoslovak economy. The Slovakian nostalgia for the economic past decreased to 64 per cent in 1998, but is still quite high, compared with other countries in Central Europe. The nostalgia for the previous economic system is consistently very high in Hungary, which is easy to explain. The majority of the Hungarian population regard the 1980s in Hungary, the regime of János Kádár, as 'the golden era' in Hungary in the twentieth century. Hence, 70 per cent of the Hungarian population express positive sentiments about the specific economic Hungarian system, which in fact was a combination of state socialism and small-scale capitalism during the 1980s.

We analyse the assessment of the population of the centrally planned economy under Communism in all eleven Central and Eastern European countries by asking the following question:

> Here is a scale for ranking how the economy works. The top, $+100$, is the best; at the bottom, -100, is the worst. Where on this scale would you put the Socialist economy?

This question represents a quantitative indicator of subjective attitudes in the form of an interval scale of retrospective satisfaction with the previous planned economy under Communism. The question measures popular support for a specific economic system. Concerning the old economic system, we can quantify the extent of support for the former centralised and bureaucratic planned economy, which had operated in most of the analysed countries for forty years, before it collapsed very quickly in 1989 (see Table 2.2). The indicator of satisfaction with the planned economy before 1989 gives the command economy a rating between $+10$ and $+100$, where $+100$ is very positive and $+10$ somewhat positive.

The overall picture concerning the past economic system for all eleven countries is one of increasing nostalgia for the economic stability of the past, when compared with the speed of economic changes and economic instability since 1989. The nostalgia for the macro-economic past went down from 61 per cent in 1996 to 60 per cent of all respondents in all ten countries – except the Federal Republic of Yugoslavia – in 1998. We can speak of an increasing nostalgia for the Communist economy between 1991 and 1994 and of a stable level of economic nostalgia around 60 per cent in Central and Eastern Europe between 1996 and 1998.

In the Russian Federation, 61 per cent of all Russians have a positive assessment of the planned economy of the Soviet Union in 1994, which is lower than the very positive evaluations of the Soviet economy in the Ukraine and in Belarus.

Nostalgia for the previous Communist government

The extent of nostalgia for the *ancien régime* under Communism in all twelve analysed countries grew between 36 per cent in 1991 and 47 per cent in 1996 in a linear manner. Between 1996 and 1998, the percentage of post-Communist citizens who show positive associations when asked about the Communist political system, remained constant at 47 per cent of the post-Communist general public in Central and South-East Europe (see Table 2.3). The patterns of general public attitudes towards the politi-

Table 2.3 Nostalgia for the former Communist government

Q. Here is a scale for ranking how the government works. The top, +100, is the best; at the bottom, −100, is the worst. Where on this scale would you put the former Communist regime?

Country	NDB 1 1991	NDB 2 1992	NDB 3 1994	NDB 4 1996	NDB 5 1998	Change 1991–8
Central Europe	39	46	40	39	41	2
Hungary	51	68	58	56	58	7
Slovakia	44	48	50	52	46	2
Slovenia	41	41	32	36	42	1
Czech Republic	23	29	23	24	31	8
Poland	34	42	38	25	30	−4
Southern Europe	28	30	37	40	41	13
FR of Yugoslavia	*	*	*	*	62	*
Bulgaria	30	42	51	58	43	13
Croatia	*	13	28	34	41	28
Romania	26	35	33	28	38	12
Northern Europe	*	*	45	46	*	1
Latvia	*	*	42	53	*	11
Lithuania	*	*	51	46	*	−5
Estonia	*	*	42	40	*	−2
Eastern Europe	*	58	60	76	71	13
Ukraine	*	55	55	75	82	27
Belarus	*	60	64	77	60	0
Russia	*	*	51	*	*	*

Notes
*Not done in this country at this time.
People with positive attitudes: +10 to +100.

cal past of Communism are quite different in Central Europe and in South-East Europe. In Central Europe, the positive thinking about the *ancien régime* reached a peak very soon in 1992 with 46 per cent of all Central Europeans having in different degrees positive evaluations of the Communist political system before 1989. Between 1992 and 1994, the group of people with positive evaluations of the *ancien régime* shrank to 40 per cent and remained at that constant level of 40 per cent until 1998. Quite to the contrary, we observe in South-East Europe a steady increase in the share of those post-Communist citizens who have positive evaluations of the former political system from 28 per cent in 1991 up to 54 per cent in 1996. Only since 1996 has the number of people thinking in a positive way about the old one-party state remained at the same level with 54 per cent in 1998.

The one and only country within the Central European buffer zone with an absolute majority of the population who evaluate the Communist one-party system in a positive way, is Hungary. This has to do with the special form of the so-called 'goulash' Communism under Secretary General János Kádár during the 1980s, a period which is seen by many Hungarians as the 'golden era' in modern Hungarian history. The nostalgia for the Hungarian former political system went up steeply at the beginning of transition from 51 per cent thinking positive about the *ancien régime* in 1991 to 68 per cent in 1992. This share of politically nostalgic Hungarians shrank to 58 per cent in 1994 and remained at that high level, if compared with other Central European countries, until 1998. In Slovakia, we witness a linear increase of positive assessments of the Communist political system between 44 per cent in 1991 and 52 per cent in 1996. Since 1996, the share of Slovaks with positive feelings about Communism in its political form went down to 46 per cent. The positive evaluation of the Yugoslav government was relatively high in Slovenia at the beginning of the transition process: in 1991 and 1992, a constant number of 41 per cent of the Slovenian population gave the former Communist government a positive rating. The Slovenian nostalgia for the *ancien régime* was quite low in 1994 and 1996, but rose again to previous levels with a share of 42 per cent in 1998. Almost throughout the whole process of political transformation in the Czech Republic, one-quarter of the Czech population displays some nostalgia for the Czechoslovak political system of the past. The widespread political depression within Czech society produced an increase of political nostalgia from 24 per cent nostalgic Czechs in 1996 to 31 per cent of the Czech population who show positive attitudes towards the Czechoslovak political past between 1948 and 1989. In Poland, we can observe the peak of political nostalgia between 1992 and 1994, when the Polish electorate was very dissatisfied with the performance of the current post-Communist government. In 1992, 42 per cent of the Polish citizens thought in a positive way about the Polish Communist government, in 1994 it was still 38 per cent who were nostalgic about the Polish *ancien régime.* Since 1994, the positive assessment of the previous Communist government in Poland is getting smaller and smaller, which coincides with growing support for the post-Communist government in Poland.

Within South-East Europe, the Ukraine is the post-Communist country with the highest level of nostalgia for the former Communist political system in comparison with all eleven other countries. In 1992, the absolute majority of 55 per cent of the Ukrainian electorate showed positive evaluations of the one-party government of the late Soviet Union. This high figure went up during the process of political transformation in a steady way and reached its peak in 1998, when 82 per cent of all Ukrainian post-Communist citizens said that they think positively about the former Communist regime. From the perspective of political stability and the future chances of democracy in the Ukraine, this figure appears to be a serious warning about the fragility of democracy and the potential risks of non-democratic alternatives eventually taking over in the Ukraine, if the political dissatisfaction of the Ukrainian electorate cannot be halted. In the Federal Republic of Yugoslavia, the nostalgia for the political system of the former Yugoslavia is, with a percentage of 62 of the Serbian electorate, quite high. This can be explained by the fact that the population of Serbia and Montenegro were at the core of the former Yugoslavia; they suffer from a post-Empire syndrome, having lost most of their former powers, resources and territories. The Byelorussian population also showed a high level of nostalgia for the Communist political system during the first half of the 1990s. At the beginning of political transition in Belarus in 1992, 60 per cent showed positive attitudes towards the political system of the Soviet Union. This share went steadily up to 77 per cent in 1996, which was almost as high as in the Ukraine at the same time. Surprisingly, the extent of nostalgia shrank from 77 per cent in 1996 to 60 per cent in 1998 in Belarus. One explanation for that different pattern in comparison with the Ukraine could be that the authoritarian regime of President Alyaksandr Lukashenka is fulfilling the basic needs of political stability by the Byelorussian public. The Lukashenka regime is in many elements very close to the previous Soviet form of government and could be seen by the Byelorussian electorate as a successful surrogate for the Communist political regime of the past. We find in the Russian Federation also a post-Empire syndrome as in Serbia, because 51 per cent of the Russians are nostalgic about the one-party government of the Soviet Union in 1994. There is a linear increase of nostalgia for the Communist political system in Bulgaria from 30 per cent in 1991 up to 58 per cent in 1996. The beginning of serious political reforms in Bulgaria since 1996 immediately reduced the nostalgia for the old political system: in 1998, only 43 per cent of the Bulgarian electorate thought positively about the Bulgarian Communist government under Secretary General Todor Zhivkov. The pattern in Croatia is very interesting. After the break-up of Yugoslavia, the Croatian electorate were very happy about the new independence and only 13 per cent of the Croatian population were nostalgic about the previous Yugoslav government. In the course of political transformation of Croatia, more and more Croats thought in a positive way about the political regime of Yugoslavia with a share of 28 per cent in 1994 and 41 per cent in 1998. This may also be a reflection of growing dissatisfaction with the incumbent Croatian central government under President Franjo Tudjman. After the traumatic experiences under President Nicolae Ceauşescu, the nostalgia for the Romanian Communist government only existed in one-quarter of the Romanian electorate with a share of 26 per cent in 1991. During the first half of the 1990s nostalgic attitudes towards the *ancien régime* in Romania remained at a constant level of one-third of the Romanian population, but between 1996 and 1998 the group of nostalgic Romanians grew from 28 per cent to 38 per cent. This also shows increasing disapproval of the current political regime in Bucharest within the Romanian electorate that creates a favourable perspective on the previous political regime.

Nostalgia for Communism as a form of political regime

We showed in the previous section that almost half of the general public in all twelve post-Communist countries analysed display positive attitudes towards the previous Communist political system. This was described as nostalgia, which shows that certain positive elements of the old system were lost during the process of transformation and that considerable parts of the societies in the post-Communist part of Europe are sad about that loss. That nostalgia does not imply, however, that half of the post-Communist societies want a restoration of Communism, wish to turn around the wheel of history and resurrect Communism as a form of non-democratic government and of a non-market economy. In order to analyse in more detail the assessment of the late system of Communism, we asked some more questions to throw more light on the complex phenomenon of nostalgia and support for restoration.

One of those questions tries to distinguish between post-Communist citizens who think that Communism was basically a 'good way of running things', that Communism was 'a good system' of organising state and government on the one hand and other respondents who have the basic attitude that Communism 'had its faults, but was basically tolerable' (see Table 2.4). The most important result was that 10 per cent of all post-Communist citizens in eleven post-Communist countries had the opinion that Communism was 'a good way of running things'. Those 10 per cent can be labelled as the core group of pro-Communist citizens in post-Communist Europe who still think in a very positive way about Communism, even almost ten years after its exit from history. This core group of Communist supporters is smaller in Central Europe, where only 7 per cent believe that Communism was a good method of running things. In

Table 2.4 Nostalgia for the Communist political regime, 1998

Q. For forty years we had a different system of government and people have different views about it. Which of these statements comes closest to expressing what you think?
A. A good way of running things.
B. Even though it had faults it was tolerable.

Country	A	B	A + B
Central Europe	10	46	56
Slovenia	8	53	61
Hungary	7	51	58
Slovakia	10	46	56
Czech Republic	4	33	37
Poland	4	32	36
Southern Europe	11	44	55
FR of Yugoslavia	18	59	77
Bulgaria	12	45	57
Croatia	5	49	54
Romania	9	23	32
Eastern Europe	14	58	72
Ukraine	16	59	75
Belarus	12	56	68

South-East Europe, the extent of a basic acceptance of Communism as a good form of government is higher than in Central Europe: 12 per cent of all post-Communist citizens in Eastern and Southern Europe are convinced that Communism is a good way of running things.

The number of strong supporters of Communism as a form of government is roughly the same in Slovakia (10 per cent), Slovenia (8 per cent) and Hungary (7 per cent). The core groups of support for Communism as a type of political system are much smaller in the Czech Republic and Hungary, with 4 per cent each in those two countries. The support for Communism as a non-democratic form of government is very high in the Federal Republic of Yugoslavia (18 per cent), but also considerable in the Ukraine (16 per cent), in Belarus (12 per cent) and in Bulgaria (12 per cent). The sympathy for a Communist political regime is somewhat lower in Romania with 9 per cent and in Croatia with 5 per cent of the electorate.

We did find a rather large group of 46 per cent of all post-Communist citizens in the eleven post-Communist societies who were convinced that Communism had 'its faults, but was nevertheless tolerable' (see Table 2.4). This group cannot be described as Communists, but as people who could live under Communism without too much dissatisfaction. Again, this group is smaller in Central Europe, where 43 per cent think about the Communist regime as one you could live with without necessarily identifying themselves with the regime and its ideological premises. This group, which is convinced that life under Communism was tolerable is with a share of 49 per cent quite higher in South-East Europe.

An absolute majority of people in Slovenia (53 per cent) and in Hungary (51 per cent) think that their own life under Communism was tolerable. In Slovakia, a majority of 46 per cent support the same statement. On the contrary, only one-third of the electorate in the Czech republic (33 per cent) and in Poland (32 per cent) think that life under Communism was tolerable; the Czechs and Poles are much more anti-Communist than the Hungarians or Slovaks for that matter. Almost 60 per cent of the general public in Serbia (59 per cent), the Ukraine (59 per cent) and in Belarus (56 per cent) find that life under the political regime of Communism was not too bad compared with their contemporary life. We did find high levels of acceptance of life under Communism in Bulgaria (45 per cent) and in Croatia (49 per cent) respectively. Only in Romania, the memory of the political regime of the Ceaușescu clan and the very specific Romanian type of Communism dampens the nostalgia for the old regime: only 23 per cent of the Romanian electorate were of the opinion that the Communist regime in Romania was tolerable.

Is there a future for Communism? Support for the restoration of Communism as a political system

In the previous section we analysed the core group of Communism as a form of government and found out that on average 10 per cent of all post-Communist citizens have the conviction that Communism is a good way to run things, a good form of government, a viable alternative to democracy. In this concluding section of Chapter 2 we analyse the question: Is Communism historically dead and has it left the stage of history forever or are there tendencies to restore Communism as a form of political and economic regime again in Europe at the level of the general public? In order to find out the extent of support for a restoration of the Communist *ancien régime*, we asked in 1994, 1996 and 1998 approximately 30,000 post-Communist citizens if it would be better to restore the former Communist regime (see Table 2.5).

The first result consists in the fact that a considerable part of post-Communist societies still believes that the Communist regime is a serious alternative to the emerging new democracies on the ruins of Communism. The idea of a restoration of Communism is not totally extinguished from the minds of people who lived between forty and seventy years under a Communist regime. In 1994, 18 per cent of all post-Communist citizens supported the idea of a Communist restoration, which increased to 21 per cent in 1996 and further to 24 per cent in 1998. This longitudinal analysis shows that the wish for a Communist restoration is not vanishing, but, on the contrary, growing during the process of political transformations and has reached now on average one-quarter of all

Table 2.5 Support for Communist restoration

Q. Do you agree or disagree: it would be better to restore the former
Communist regime?

Country	NDB 3 1994	NDB 4 1996	NDB 5 1998	Change 1994–8
Central Europe	14	14	19	5
Slovakia	16	19	29	13
Hungary	18	20	23	5
Czech Republic	7	9	16	9
Poland	18	8	14	−4
Slovenia	12	12	14	2
Southern Europe	15	16	19	4
FR of Yugoslavia	*	*	30	*
Bulgaria	25	29	24	−1
Romania	12	12	19	7
Croatia	8	6	14	6
Northern Europe	6	7	*	1
Lithuania	8	7	*	−1
Estonia	5	7	*	2
Latvia	6	6	*	0
Eastern Europe	30	46	42	12
Ukraine	25	43	51	26
Belarus	34	49	33	−1
Russia	23	*	*	*

Notes
*Not done in this country at this time.
Percentage of persons who definitely or somewhat agree.

post-Communist citizens in all twelve societies in Central and South-East
Europe analysed in 1998. The desire for a return to Communism is
weaker in Central Europe and stronger in South-East Europe. In Central
Europe the share of supporters for a Communist renaissance was constantly at 14 per cent between 1994 and 1996, but increased to 19 per cent
in 1998. In South-East Europe, the extent of support for replacing democracy by the old political system of Communism grew from 21 per cent in
1994 to 28 per cent in 1996. Fortunately, this share of 28 per cent of
people wanting the return of Communism remained stable between 1996
and 1998 and did not grow overall in the Eastern and Southern parts of
Europe.

Within Central Europe, the desire to return to Communism is highest
in Slovakia. In 1994, only 16 per cent supported the return of Communism, whereas this figure increased to 19 per cent in 1996 and finally to 29
per cent in 1998. The astonishing fact is that we find that almost one-third
of the Slovak electorate in the middle of the Central European buffer
zone support the return of Communism as a political regime. We will see
if the change of government of Slovakia and the end of the 'Meciar era' in
the second half of 1998 will reduce this widespread desire to return to

Communism and strengthen the young Slovak democracy. In Hungary, we have a constant fifth of the Hungarian electorate who are dissatisfied with the new Hungarian democracy and want to go back to the Hungarian version of Communism, which existed during the 1980s. In the Czech Republic, the support for a return to Communism was very low in 1994 (7 per cent) and in 1996 (9 per cent). The political crisis in the second half of the 1990s in the Czech Republic produced a high level of political dissatisfaction and an unexpected rise in support for a return to Communism with a share of 16 per cent of the Czech electorate. In Poland, the pattern over time was exactly the reverse if compared with the Czech pattern. The support for a return of Communism as a political regime was highest at the beginning of political transformations with the extreme fragmentation of the Polish party system and hence with the Polish parliament: in 1994, 18 per cent of the Polish population were fed up with the young Polish democracy and wanted a return to Communism in Poland. This share of Polish anti-democrats decreased over time and is now at a level of 14 per cent. In Slovenia, a constant group between 10 and 15 per cent of the general public favour a return to the Yugoslavian model of Communism without any clear-cut pattern over time.

Once again, the Ukraine is the country with the greatest extent of anti-democratic attitudes of the general public in comparison with the eleven other post-Communist societies. In 1994, only 25 per cent of the Ukrainian population supported the idea of going back to Communism. Unfortunately, this desire for a return to Communism reached 43 per cent in 1996 and finally 51 per cent of the Ukrainian electorate in 1998. The Ukraine is the one and only country in post-Communist Europe where an absolute majority supports the actual return of Communism, which appears to be quite a strong indicator of an extremely high level of discontent with the actual political system in the Ukraine, and an indicator of the risk of a collapse of democracy and market economy in this country with all the potential consequences of such a break-down and of the possible attempt to reinstate Communism. Again, the longitudinal pattern in Belarus is different in comparison to the Ukraine. As in the Ukraine, the desire for a return to Communism increased from 34 per cent in 1994 to 49 per cent in 1996. But, contrary to the Ukraine, the support for a Communist restoration in Belarus fell from 49 per cent in 1996 quite steeply to 33 per cent in 1998! This might be explained either by the acceptance of the political regime of President Lukashenka or by the conviction of the Byelorussian electorate that a return to Communism will not improve the political condition in Belarus to such an extent that it is worth the risk of such a reverse transformation from democracy to Communism. In Serbia and Montenegro, 30 per cent of the population want a return to a 'Tito-style Yugoslavia', which appears to be part of the Serbian 'post-Empire syndrome'. In Bulgaria, we find a constant share of one-quarter of the Bulgarian electorate who express their hope of a return of Communism.

In 1994, 23 per cent of all Russians supported a return to Communism as a political regime as existed in the Soviet Union before the breakdown of that empire. In Romania, we find a constant group of 12 per cent of the electorate in 1994 and 1996 who favoured the return of Romanian Communism. The disappointment of large parts of Romanian society with the progress of political transformations resulted in an increase to 19 per cent of the Romanian population who supported the return of Romanian Communism as a form of regime in 1998. The desire for a return to the Communist Yugoslavia was very rare in the newly founded state of Croatia. In 1994, only 8 per cent supported the return to Communism and in 1996 even less, 6 per cent, were in favour of a Communist restoration. The growing discontent with the political regime under President Tudjman resulted in the fact that 14 per cent of the Croatian population supported a return to Communism in Croatia in 1998.

3 The birth of democracy

Support for the new political regime in post-Communism

When we measure support for the new political regime, we do not measure any abstract concept of democracy, but the assessment of the current political system, the current political regime in a given post-Communist society. We analyse the reaction of the post-Communist citizen to the form and structure of a more or less democratic system, which he or she is experiencing in their native land. The concept of support for democracy was operationalised by the following question:

> Here is a scale for ranking how the government works. The top, +100, is the best; at the bottom, −100, is the worst. Where on this scale would you put the current regime?

For the purposes of the analysis in this section, we selected only people who gave the current democratic system an evaluation in the range between +10 and +100 on the democracy scale. The support for democracy is quite different in Central Europe in comparison with South-East Europe (see Table 3.1). All over the post-Communist world, we noticed a high level of euphoria about democracy and its prospects at the very beginning of political transformation with the highest levels of support for democracy during the whole period between 1991 and 1998. An average of 53 per cent in eight post-Communist countries gave democracy a positive evaluation in 1991, in Central Europe 56 per cent supported democracy and 67 per cent of South-East Europeans thought that democracy was a good thing in 1991. Quite to the contrary, we find that only 14 per cent of the Russian electorate supported the new Russian regime immediately after the demise of the Soviet Union in 1991. Between 1991 and 1998, an average of 52 per cent of all post-Communist citizens in twelve post-Communist countries supported the new democracy, thus giving democracy an absolute majority in the first decade of transition.

Table 3.1 Support for the current government

Q. Here is a scale for ranking how the government works. The top, +100, is the best; at the bottom, −100, is the worst. Where on this scale would you put the current regime?

Country	NDB 1 1991	NDB 2 1992	NDB 3 1994	NDB 4 1996	NDB 5 1998	Change 1991–8
Central Europe	56	59	61	66	55	−1
Poland	52	56	69	76	66	14
Czech Republic	71	71	78	77	56	−15
Hungary	57	43	51	50	53	−4
Slovenia	49	68	55	66	51	2
Slovakia	50	58	52	61	50	0
Southern Europe	67	56	57	57	46	−21
Romania	69	68	60	60	66	−3
Bulgaria	64	55	59	66	58	−6
FR of Yugoslavia	*	*	*	*	33	*
Croatia	*	44	51	44	27	−17
Northern Europe	*	*	48	45	*	*
Estonia	*	*	67	61	*	−6
Lithuania	*	*	35	39	*	4
Latvia	*	*	43	34	*	−9
Eastern Europe	14	32	39	31	35	21
Belarus	*	35	29	35	48	13
Russia	14	36	48	26	36	24
Ukraine	*	25	24	33	22	−3

Notes
* Not done in this country at this time.
People with positive attitudes: +10 to +100.

In Central Europe, democracy was able to get deeper roots and increasing support in the course of transition. The support for Central European democracy went up to 59 per cent in 1992 and increased even further to 61 per cent in 1994 and 66 per cent in 1996. Hence we might argue that support for democracy grew between 1991 and 1996 in a steady and linear way in Central Europe within the general public of that European region, encompassing finally 66 per cent of all Central Europeans, which appears to be quite an impressive birth of democracy in such a short period of time, if one thinks about other processes of democratisation during the first and second wave of democratisation. Nevertheless, we witnessed a drop of support for Central European democracy from 66 per cent in 1996 to 55 per cent in 1998. In the period between 1991 and 1998, on average an absolute majority of 59 per cent of Central Europeans were in favour of democracy.

In the Balkans, on the other hand, the euphoria of 1991 was replaced by a rather stable realism about the situation and the prospects of democracy in that part of Europe during the period of transition from totalitarianism to democracy. We find a constant majority between 46 and 57 per cent of the Southern Europeans who evaluate their own new democracy in a positive way. In comparison across time and across region, we find that between 1991 and 1998, on average a majority of 57 per cent of all post-Communist citizens in Southern Europe supported democracy.

In Eastern Europe, the support for the new regime is lowest compared to the other two regions of transition. Between 1991 and 1994, we notice an increase of support for the current regime from 14 per cent up to 39 per cent. Since 1994, only about one-third of the electorate in post-Communist Eastern Europe can be regarded as supporting the new political regime, which is extremely low in comparison with Central Europe and Southern Europe.

Within Central Europe, the country with the highest actual support for the new democracy is Poland. At the beginning of the Polish process of political transformation towards democracy, in 1991, a majority of 52 per cent of the Polish electorate supported the new political system. This group of Polish democrats grew to 56 per cent in 1992 and to 69 per cent in 1994. The peak of support for democracy was reached in 1996, when 76 per cent of the Polish population showed positive evaluations of the young Polish democracy. Between 1996 and 1998, the positive assessment of the current political system in Poland decreased from 76 per cent to 66 per cent. Nevertheless, this share of 66 per cent of the Polish general public represents the greatest group of democrats, if one compares Poland with other Central European countries in the most recent New Democracies Barometer survey in 1998. The Czech Republic was the model country concerning the political transformation towards a pluralist democracy between 1991 and 1996. During that period, a record share of between 71 and 78 per cent of the Czech electorate gave the young second Czech democracy positive ratings, thus showing by far the greatest support for a new democracy among all twelve post-Communist countries analysed. The considerable political crisis in Czech politics in 1997 and 1998, which ended in the change from the incumbent government under the Conservative Prime Minister Vacláv Klaus to a new government under a Social Democratic Prime Minister Milos Zeman, produced the first and steep drop of support for the Czech political system after 1989. The share of satisfied Czech democrats fell from 76 per cent in 1986 to 56 per cent in 1998, which represents a decrease of 20 percentage points within two years. The peaceful change of Czech government in 1998 showed also that the young Czech democracy fulfilled a basic requirement of democratic rule that the people in any democracy are able to 'throw the rascals out', when they are dissatisfied and have the power to try another government. This political crisis in the second half of the 1990s was responsible for the Czech democracy losing her leading position and allowing the Polish democracy to take the lead in 1998 within Central Europe. In Hungary the pattern of the birth of democracy is quite different in comparison to Poland or the Czech Republic. At the very beginning of transition towards democracy, the Hungarian electorate was very positive about the new political system. In 1991, an absolute majority of 57 per cent of all Hungarians supported the new democracy in Hungary, a value which was never achieved since. Between 1991 and 1992, we notice a steep decline for democratic support from 57 to 43 per cent of the Hungarian electorate. Hungarian support for democracy recovered until 1994 to 51 per cent and oscillated between 1994 and 1998 at a constant level between 50 and 53 per cent of the Hungarian population. Despite the widespread perceptions of 'Hungarian pessimism', we can hypothesise that the absolute majority of the Hungarian general public supports the new democracy and rejects all alternative forms of non-democratic regimes. Hungarian support for democracy is almost as high as the Czech support for democracy and higher than the level of democratic support in Slovenia and Slovakia in 1998. The pattern of democratic support is very volatile in Slovenia. The share of Slovenian democrats oscillates throughout the whole period between 49 and 68 per cent of the Slovenian electorate. The share of Slovenians who give the Slovenian democracy positive ratings fell from 66 per cent in 1996 to 51 per cent in 1998. Whatever the fluctuations and their reasons, it is important to state that an absolute majority of the Slovenian electorate backs the new democracy in Slovenia in the most recent New Democracy Barometer survey in 1998. The pattern in Slovakia is very similar to the pattern in Slovenia with frequent oscillations of democratic support in the range between 50 and 61 per cent of the Slovak electorate. The level of satisfaction with the new Slovak democracy decreased from 61 per cent in 1996 to 50 per cent in summer 1998 at the end of the era of Prime Minister Vladimir Meciar, showing a considerable level of dissatisfaction with the political regime under the government of Vladimir Meciar. This obvious dissatisfaction of the Slovak electorate yielded the victory of the anti-Meciar coalition in autumn 1998 and produced the new Slovak coalition government under Prime Minister Dzurinda.

Within Southern Europe, the country with by far the greatest support for the new government is Romania. At the beginning of the process of political transformation towards democracy in 1991 and 1992, we find a record level of democratic euphoria in Romania with 69 and 68 per cent of the Romanian electorate supporting the young Romanian government and being relieved after the nightmare of the Ceausescu regime. After the cooling down of democratic euphoria in 1991 and 1992, the level of democratic support fell somewhat to 60 per cent in 1994 as well as in 1996. The positive rating of the incumbent government in Romania grew from 60 per cent in 1996 to 66 per cent in 1998, which reflects the positive reactions of the Romanian population to the change in Romanian government in 1996 to Prime Minister Konstantinesco. In Bulgaria, there was a euphoric hope in the new democratic system at the beginning of political transformation in 1991, when 64 per cent of all Bulgarians thought positively about the new Bulgarian democracy. Two years after the first Bulgarian election with a victory for the Bulgarian Socialist Party (BSP), approval for the new political system fell from 64 per cent in 1991 to 55 per cent in 1992. Since 1992, we have witnessed a steady increase of support for democracy in Bulgaria to 59 per cent in 1994 and 66 per cent in 1996. Whereas support for democracy grew between 1996 and 1998 in Romania, we see a reverse trend in Bulgaria: after the peak of democratic support in 1996, the number of Bulgarians who have a positive evaluation of the new Bulgarian political system fell to 58 per cent in 1998. This falling approval rate of Bulgarian democracy seems to be due to growing dissatisfaction with the current government in Bulgaria.

Only one-third of Serbs and Montenegrinians (33 per cent) support the political system under President Milosevic in the Federal Republic of Yugoslavia in 1998. The approval rate for the political system in the newly created Croatia increased from 44 per cent in 1992 to 51 per cent in 1994, at the beginning of the political transformation. Since 1994, the support for the Croatian political regime has fallen to 44 per cent in 1996 and 27 per cent in 1998. This linear decline of support for the new Croatian political system indicates increasing dissatisfaction of the Croatian population with the political regime under President Tudjman in the course of the last four years.

In Belarus, we find a growing number of people who think positively about the current political regime between 1994 and 1998. In 1994, only 29 per cent of the Byelorussians gave the political system a positive evaluation; this rating went up to 35 per cent in 1996 and finally to 48 per cent in 1998. Hence, we can argue that a relative majority of the Byelorussian electorate give the current political regime under President Lukashenka in Belarus, which is not fulfilling the criteria for a pluralist democracy, a positive rating. In the Russian Federation, more than one-third of the Russian citizens support the new Russian regime throughout the period between 1991 and 1998, which is less than in Belarus and more than in the Ukraine. In 1998, 36 per cent of the Russian electorate give the current regime a positive evaluation, which means on the other hand that more than 60 per cent of the Russian people are dissatisfied with the way democracy works in 1998. In the latter, the support for the new political system is consistently low throughout the whole period of observation. The approval rate for the Ukrainian political system oscillates between 22 and 33 per cent without any clear-cut pattern over time, showing a constantly low level of satisfaction with how democracy works in the Ukraine.

Future of democratic national parliaments

An important factor for the stability and the future of parliamentary democracy is the support for the national parliament in an emerging democratic system. Is there already a visible readiness to support and protect parliament, if attacked by non-democratic forces or is the national parliament as a crucial element of a pluralist democracy not yet embedded within the population?

An important indicator of the future chances of survival of a new democracy is the expectation within a national electorate that the national parliament could be suspended in the next few years. If a growing number of people do not expect that their parliament will be dissolved and replaced by some non-democratic institution, we can hypothesise that the chances of democracy surviving are also growing (see Table 3.2). The most important outcome of the empirical analysis consists in the fact that during the process of democratic transition, more and more post-Communist citizens are convinced that the national parliament will not be suspended in the near future, that is, parliament in particular and democracy in general will survive in their own country in the foreseeable future. At the beginning of democratic transition in 1991, only 62 per cent of all post-Communist citizens said it was unlikely that their national parliament would be suspended, which means that almost 40 per cent were anxious about the possibility of an attack on parliament two years after the end of Communism. Optimism about the future prospects of national parliaments as

Table 3.2 Expectations about the future of the democratic national parliament

Q. Some people think this country would be better governed if parliament were suspended and we did not have lots of political parties. How likely do you think it is that this could happen here in the next few years?

Country	NDB 1 1991	NDB 2 1992	NDB 3 1994	NDB 4 1996	NDB 5 1998	Change 1991–8
Central Europe	59	66	64	68	83	24
Poland	44	40	47	38	90	46
Hungary	75	76	71	75	90	15
Slovenia	60	81	64	83	85	25
Czech Republic	61	64	72	80	80	19
Slovakia	53	67	65	66	72	19
Southern Europe	69	69	67	75	77	8
Bulgaria	70	66	63	74	91	21
FR of Yugoslavia	*	*	*	*	73	*
Croatia	*	67	69	73	71	4
Romania	68	73	69	77	70	2
Northern Europe	*	*	61	76	*	15
Lithuania	*	*	60	85	*	25
Estonia	*	*	71	80	*	9
Latvia	*	*	51	63	*	12
Eastern Europe	*	59	55	69	73	14
Ukraine	*	60	51	58	75	15
Belarus	*	57	51	64	73	16
Russia	*	*	62	84	70	8

Notes
* Not done in this country at this time.
Percentage of people saying suspension of parliament is unlikely.

central post-Communist institutions grew to 65 per cent in 1992, but fell again in 1994 to the initial level of 62 per cent. Since 1994, however, the number of post-Communist citizens who believe in the survival of their national parliaments is steadily increasing. We witness a growing optimism to a share of 70 per cent in 1996 and finally to a record level of 78 per cent of all post-Communist citizens in twelve countries in 1998. This phenomenon shows the growing basis of support for parliamentary democracy in post-Communist Europe.

In Central Europe, the considerable growth of optimism about the survival of parliament is visible and goes from 59 per cent in 1991 up to 68 per cent in 1996 and 83 per cent in 1998. This shows the strengthening of the parliamentary roots of the new democracies in the Central European buffer zone in an impressive manner. The expectations about a possible suspension of the national parliament were quite stable in Southern Europe in the period between 1991 and 1994 with figures between 67 and 69 per cent being optimistic about the chances for the national parliament. It is important to note that between 1994 and 1998, the optimism about the survival of democratic parliaments grew in a steady manner in Southern Europe. In 1998, we find on average 83 per cent of parliamentary optimists in Central Europe and 77 per cent of parliamentary optimists in Southern Europe, which indicates convergent longitudinal patterns between those two different regions of post-Communist change. As in Central and Southern Europe, we find also in Eastern Europe the lowest level of expectations for the survival of a democratic parliament in 1994, when only 55 per cent of East Europeans thought that their parliament was not under threat of being dissolved in the near future.

The Polish electorate were quite sceptical about the future chances of the *Sejm* between 1991 and 1996 with a low share of optimists oscillating between 38 per cent in 1996 and 47 per cent in 1994. After years of instability and uncertainty, which several times looked very bleak, we find 90 per cent optimistic about the Polish parliament in 1998, which indicates a late stabilisation of parliamentary democracy in Poland, which at the same time is pushing the young Polish democracy at the first rank concerning this indicator of democratisation among the Central European political systems. In Hungary, the group optimistic about the future of the Hungarian parliament was at a constant level between 71 and 76 per cent throughout the whole period from 1991 to 1996 within a clear direction. As in Poland, we find a final swing towards strong confidence in the survival of parliamentary democracy in Hungary in 1998, when 90 per cent of the Hungarian electorate say that it is unlikely that the national parliament will be suspended in the foreseeable future. The optimism about the survival of the Slovenian parliament is volatile at the beginning of transition and oscillating between 60 per cent and 81 per cent in the period between 1991 and 1994. Optimism grew from 64 per cent in 1994 to 83 per cent in 1996 and since then has remained at this high level with 85 per cent in 1998. In the Czech Republic we found a clear pattern of increasing optimism about the future and persistence of the Czech parliament from 61 per cent in 1991 to 64 per cent in 1992 and 72 per cent in 1994. Since 1994, a constant share of 80 per cent of the Czech electorate is convinced that any non-democratic institution will not suspend the Czech national parliament, indicating also a shift towards a consolidation of Czech democracy in the period 1996 to 1998. There was a considerable degree of scepticism about the survival of parliamentary democracy at the beginning of the political transformations in Slovakia in 1991, when only 53 per cent of the Slovak population were optimistic that the Slovak parliament would not be suspended in the future. Between 1992 and 1996, we find a constant level of 65 to 67 per cent of the Slovak electorate who are optimistic about the future prospects of the Slovak national parliament. In 1998, we see a step towards consolidation of parliamentary democracy in Slovakia too. Despite the political turbulences in the last two years of the government under Prime Minister Meciar, the Slovak population was quite optimistic that no political force would suspend the national parliament. This expectation was confirmed by the peaceful change of government in autumn 1998 in Slovakia from Prime Minister Meciar to Prime Minister Dzurinda.

The results for Central Europe form a strong empirical and comparative evidence that with regard to parliamentary democracy we can define the years between 1989 and 1996 as the first period of 'transition towards democracy' from the Communist political system to parliamentary democracy, whereas 1998 appears to be the starting point of the second period of political transformation, which could be characterised as the period of 'consolidation of democracy' in the post-Communist part of Europe.

The analysis of the expectations of survival of the national parliament in Southern Europe clearly shows that 1994 can be regarded as the critical year in that respect. In all countries of that European region where we have longitudinal data, the pattern is the same with the exception of Croatia, which until recently can be labelled as a society at war and hence represents a deviant case. The optimism about the survival of the national parliament shrank everywhere in Southern Europe between 1991 and 1994. In 1994, many post-Communist citizens in that region were not so sure, whether the young democracy would survive and not lose against some other form of non-democratic regime. Fortunately for Europe in general and for the Southern Europeans in particular, this crisis of confidence in the continuity of young democracies in post-Communism in 1994 did not persist and was slowly replaced by growing optimism about the future of parliamentary democracy.

In Bulgaria, an absolute majority of 70 per cent were convinced at the beginning of political transition that the new Bulgarian parliament would survive the next years to come. Unfortunately, that share of optimism decreased to 66 per cent in 1992 and finally to 51 per cent in 1994. Since

1994, we have noticed in Bulgaria a steep increase in parliamentary optimists to 74 per cent in 1996 and 91 per cent in 1998, which is as high as the leading countries in Central Europe, Poland and Hungary. The empirical impression is that Bulgaria has reached the point of no return to the previous political system finally in 1998, when more than 90 per cent of the Bulgarian electorate think that the Bulgarian parliament will not be suspended in the future and substituted by whatever non-democratic institution with legislative powers. The process of political transformation in Bulgaria is very interesting, because it shows the difference between basic support for democracy and its institutions as a whole, on the one hand, and approval or disapproval with the government and the political system of the day, on the other. Despite strong discontent by the Bulgarian electorate with certain governments, certain parties and other elements of current political life in Bulgaria, the Bulgarians believe more and more that parliamentary democracy will stay in Bulgaria, that the general legitimacy of the new democratic political system is broadening and deepening. We find exactly the same level of confidence with a share of 73 per cent who expect that the national parliament will not be suspended in the future in the Federal Republic of Yugoslavia in 1998. The level of optimism about the survival of the national parliament is constant over time in Croatia, where between 67 and 73 per cent of the Croatian population expect that anti-democratic forces will not suspend the Croatian *Sabor*. As in Croatia, we find a constant level of optimism about the future positive prospects of the Romanian parliament with a range between 68 and 77 per cent.

The striking contrast between actual political discontent and general support for parliamentary democracy can be found in the Ukraine, where this difference is even bigger. The share of Ukrainian optimists with regard to the survival of the Ukrainian parliament went down from 60 per cent in 1992 to 51 per cent in 1994, which again can be seen as the critical year in the transformation from Communism to democracy, when the outcome of the political process was extremely uncertain. Since 1994 the share of optimists concerning the survival chances of the Ukrainian parliament went up to 58 per cent in 1996 and finally reached 75 per cent in 1998, which is somewhat lower than the average in Central Europe, but nevertheless quite high compared to many other political indicators in the Ukraine, which show massive dissatisfaction with the actual political life in the Ukraine. The Ukrainian general public obviously expects the national parliament to persist in the long term in spite of the deep structural crisis of Ukrainian politics at the end of the 1990s. We find the same pattern as in the Ukraine in Belarus too. In 1992, an absolute majority of 60 per cent of the Byelorussian electorate were optimistic about the future prospects of the national parliament in Minsk. That share of optimists fell to 51 per cent in 1994, again showing 1994 as the critical year regarding this dimension of general support for the new political system. Since 1994, the group of optimists for the survival of the Byelorussian parliament grew again to

64 per cent in 1996 and 73 per cent in 1998. In Russia, finally, only 62 per cent of the inhabitants of the Russian Federation were optimistic about the chances of the *Duma* to survive the political crisis in Russia in the foreseeable future. This group of Russian optimists grew to 84 per cent in 1996 and reached 70 per cent in 1998, which is somewhat lower than the average for post-Communist Eastern Europe.

Popular support for democratic national parliaments

After describing the expectations of the post-Communist general public concerning the mid-term survival of democratic national parliaments, we now turn to the discussion of how deeply the newly created national parliaments are already embedded in the political value system of the different national populations. We measure this phenomenon by asking if the respondent would approve or disapprove personally the undemocratic suspension of the national parliament (see Table 3.3). From a longitudinal perspective, we do find an interesting pattern in all twelve post-Communist countries taken together. The share of post-Communist citizens who were against suspension of a democratically elected parlia-

Table 3.3 Extent of support for the national parliament

Q. If parliament was suspended and parties abolished, would you approve or disapprove?

Country	NDB 1 1991	NDB 2 1992	NDB 3 1994	NDB 4 1996	NDB 5 1998	Change 1991–8
Central Europe	80	76	75	77	78	−2
Hungary	75	75	70	74	83	8
Poland	67	57	71	68	81	14
Czech Republic	88	78	82	85	78	10
Slovakia	85	81	76	78	77	−8
Slovenia	85	89	*	81	73	−12
Southern Europe	85	82	77	83	76	−9
Croatia	*	94	80	82	88	−6
Bulgaria	79	72	75	78	77	−2
Romania	90	81	76	88	72	−18
FR of Yugoslavia	*	*	*	*	67	*
Northern Europe	*	*	58	72	*	14
Estonia	*	*	70	78	*	8
Lithuania	*	*	55	77	*	22
Latvia	*	*	50	60	*	10
Eastern Europe	*	63	51	53	63	0
Belarus	*	68	57	60	72	4
Russia	*	*	40	61	62	22
Ukraine	*	58	56	39	55	−3

Notes
* Not done in this country at this time.
Percentage people disapproving of suspension of parliament.

ment was very high at the beginning of democratic transition in 1991, when on average 81 per cent of all post-Communist citizens disapproved of the suspension of their national parliaments. This share of people defending the new national parliament decreased to 75 per cent in 1992 and 68 per cent in 1994, which represented the lowest level during the whole transition period. Here again, we see that 1994 is a year of crisis and a real milestone in political transformation. In the period between 1994 and 1998, we can speak of a process of steadily growing support for national parliaments all over post-Communist Europe. After touching the bottom of support in 1994, the share of supporters of parliaments went up to 72 per cent in 1996 and finally to 74 per cent in 1998.

In Central Europe we find a constant level of support for the newly created national parliaments in that region with shares in the range between 75 and 80 per cent of all post-Communist citizens in the buffer zone, which is the most advanced in that aspect of political life too. In Southern Europe, the backing of parliaments decreased from a record level of 85 per cent in 1991 to 82 per cent in 1992 and 77 per cent in 1994. The legitimacy of parliaments recovered to 83 per cent in 1996, but fell again in 1998 because of the low level of parliamentary legitimacy in the Federal Republic of Yugoslavia. The legitimacy of the new national parliaments is lowest in Eastern Europe: it fell from 63 per cent in 1992 to 51 per cent in 1994, which is in that region also the year of political crisis. But even at a very low level, support for the democratic parliaments increased slowly in Eastern Europe to 53 per cent in 1996 and 63 per cent in 1998, which shows the slow development of roots of parliamentary legitimacy even in that least developed part of post-Communist Europe.

We find the greatest extent of legitimacy of the national parliament in Hungary, where the overwhelming majority of 83 per cent would disapprove of a suspension of the Hungarian parliament by non-democratic forces. During the period 1991 to 1996 the level of support for the Hungarian democratic parliament was consistently between 70 and 75 per cent of the Hungarian electorate. This leading position of Hungary regarding the general legitimacy of the national parliament contradicts the widespread stereotype that the Hungarian population expresses low levels of satisfaction with the new democracy in opinion polls, which is used very often as an argument against quantitative survey research as a method of comparative political science. Poland ranks second concerning the level of parliamentary legitimacy within the Central European buffer zone. The support for the Polish *Sejm* started very low with 67 per cent in 1991, which was extremely low compared with the other emerging Central European democracies. This small extent of legitimacy shrank even more to 57 per cent in 1992, which was the crisis year in support for the Polish national parliament, somewhat earlier than the classical year of political crisis in post-Communist Europe, 1994. Since 1992 the legitimacy of the Polish *Sejm* has increased to 71 per cent in 1994 and made a big leap forward to

81 per cent in 1998, which indicates the final consolidation of general support for the Polish national parliament. In the Czech Republic, we find a very high level of parliamentary legitimacy throughout the whole period of political transition in a range between 78 and 88 per cent of the Czech population. The recent political crisis resulted in a decrease of support for the Czech parliament from 85 per cent in 1996 to 78 per cent in 1998, but only reflects short-term dissatisfaction by the Czech electorate with current Czech politics. In Slovakia, there is a high level of legitimacy of the Slovak parliament at the beginning of transition in 1991 (85 per cent) and 1992 (81 per cent). The political process afterwards resulted in a consistently lower level of support for the Slovak parliament with shares between 76 and 78 per cent in the period between 1994 and 1998. In Slovenia, the general support for the national parliament is very volatile. The Slovenian electorate backed their parliament with oscillating values between 73 and 89 per cent and displayed a very low level of support in 1998. The tendency of support for the Slovenian national parliament fell during the processes of political transition between 1991 and 1998.

The readiness of the Croatian public to defend the *Sabor* is consistently very high in comparison with other political systems in Central and Southern Europe. In 1992, the record number of 94 per cent of the Croatian electorate expressed their support for the Croatian parliament against any non-democratic threat. In 1994, this share decreased to 80 per cent and to 82 per cent in 1996, but we find with 88 per cent of the Croatian general public again an extremely high level of legitimacy of the Croatian national parliament in 1998. In Bulgaria, the support for the national parliament is rather constant over time. The support for the Bulgarian parliament is within a range between 72 and 79 per cent throughout the whole period of political transition. At the beginning of transition, we find very high levels of support for the Romanian parliament in 1991, when 90 per cent of the Romanian electorate disapproved of any attempt to dissolve the new parliament. This high legitimacy of the Romanian parliament sank to 81 per cent in 1992 and to 76 per cent in 1994, showing 1994 again as the year of political crisis. Until 1996, support for the new Romanian legislature went up to 88 per cent, but decreased since to 72 per cent in 1998. The parliament of the Federal Republic of Yugoslavia is only supported by 67 per cent of the Serbian and Montenegrinian population, which indicates a certain weakness of political legitimacy of the Yugoslav parliament.

Within Eastern Europe, the highest level of legitimacy of the new national parliament can be found in Belarus: in 1992, an absolute majority of the Byelorussian population were against the non-democratic suspension of the national parliament. This figure went down to 57 per cent in 1994, which was in Belarus the year of lowest legitimacy too. Since 1994, however, support for the Byelorussian parliament against suspension has grown to 60 per cent in 1996 and finally to 72 per cent in 1998, which is the same level as in Romania in the late 1990s. The backing of the Russian

Duma against non-democratic attacks was very low in 1994, when only 40 per cent of the Russians disapproved of a potential coup against the 'White House' in Moscow. The legitimacy of the Russian *Duma* has improved since 1994: in 1996, 61 per cent of the Russian electorate supported the *Duma* as a political institution of the new Russia and 62 per cent of the Russian general public gave the Russian parliament general legitimacy in 1998, despite the general political crisis. The lowest extent of popular support for the national parliament in a comparison of all twelve post-Communist countries can be found in the Ukraine. The support for the Ukrainian national parliament had, in addition to that, a downward tendency between 1992 and 1996: in 1992, an absolute majority of 58 per cent of all Ukrainians were prepared to defend the national parliament against non-democratic coups. This figure sank to 56 per cent in 1994 and to 39 per cent in 1996, which represents the lowest figure of general support for a national parliament over all post-Communist Europe. Since the dangerously low extent of popular support for the Ukrainian parliament recovered slightly to 55 per cent in 1998, which again is by far the lowest level of legitimacy of any post-Communist new parliament in post-Communist Europe, and could be a cause of concern about the future development of the Ukrainian political system after the turn of the century.

Alternatives to democracy: support for an authoritarian leader

The birth of democracy and the consolidation of democracy are closely linked to the availability and acceptance of alternatives to democracy. In this section we analyse the extent and structure of popular support for a 'strong and authoritarian leader' in post-Communism (see Table 3.4). The main result of our research consists in the fact that the support for a strong leader, which replaces the pluralist democracy by the rule of one man, is melting away during the course of transition from Communist dictatorship to pluralist democracy. At an early stage of political transformations – in 1992 – an absolute majority of post-Communist citizens, especially in Southern and Eastern Europe, of 58 per cent were in favour of a strong leader replacing the new democracy. In all twelve countries, that support for a strong politician decreased to one-third of all post-Communist citizens (33 per cent) in 1994 and went down further to 29 per cent in 1996. This linear decline of support for a one-man dictatorship replacing democracy carried on until 1998, when only 25 per cent of all post-Communist citizens were in favour of a non-democratic dictatorship of one person, which is normally expected to be a man. The lowest level of support for the non-democratic rule of one leader we find in Central Europe with 27 per cent in 1992 and 1994 respectively. The group of supporters of one-man dictatorship within Central Europe decreased

Table 3.4 Alternatives to democracy: support for a strong authoritarian leader

Q. Do you agree or disagree with the view that it is best to get rid of Parliament and elections and have a strong leader who can quickly decide things?

Country	NDB 2 1992	NDB 3 1994	NDB 4 1996	NDB 5 1998	Change 1992–8
Central Europe	27	27	23	19	−8
Poland	31	35	33	28	−3
Slovakia	24	24	19	23	−1
Hungary	27	18	21	18	−9
Slovenia	*	42	29	14	−28
Czech Republic	24	16	12	13	−11
Southern Europe	47	28	19	20	−27
Bulgaria	66	45	22	29	−37
Romania	27	30	29	27	0
FR of Yugoslavia	*	*	*	12	*
Croatia	*	9	5	11	2
Northern Europe	*	*	44	51	7
Lithuania	*	*	57	61	4
Latvia	*	*	37	49	12
Estonia	*	*	37	44	7
Eastern Europe	65	49	62	43	−22
Ukraine	53	56	67	55	2
Belarus	76	57	56	37	−39
Russia	*	33	*	36	3

Notes
* Not done in this country at this time.
Percentage people agreeing.

further to 23 per cent in 1996 and finally to 19 per cent in 1998. The initial support for one strong man on top of a non-democratic political system was, with 47 per cent in Southern Europe, much higher in comparison with Central Europe. The preference for a one-man political system went down to 28 per cent in 1994 and remained at the level of one-fifth of Southern Europeans in 1996 (19 per cent) and 1998 (20 per cent). Hence, we can hypothesise that one-fifth of the post-Communist citizens in Central Europe as well in Southern Europe are in favour of a one-man rule as an alternative to democracy nine years after the end of Communism, in 1998. The greatest extent of public support for a strong authoritarian leader instead of democracy we find in Eastern Europe, where an average of 65 per cent did support this alternative to democracy at an early stage of transition, in 1992. Hence, we can postulate that democracy as a form of government was in a minority position until 1996 in the three countries of the former Soviet Union which we are analysing.

Within Central Europe, Poland is the country with the highest level of support for a strong non-democratic leader. In 1992, 31 per cent of the Polish electorate were in favour of a strong leader, which even increased to 35 per cent in 1994. Since the critical year of 1994, the group of Polish citizens in favour of a one-man rule has shrunk steadily to 33 per cent in 1996 and finally to 28 per cent in 1998. In Slovakia, a constant group of one-quarter of the Slovak population is in favour of one strong man replacing democracy during the whole time period without a clear-cut tendency over time. In Hungary, support for a strong authoritarian leader was quite high with 27 per cent of the Hungarian electorate at the beginning of political transition. Since 1992, the share of Hungarians who are in favour of this non-democratic alternative sank to one-fifth of the population and remained at this level between 1994 and 1998. The alternative of a one-man government without democracy was quite high with 42 per cent in Slovenia in the critical year 1994, but fell steeply to 29 per cent in 1996 and went down further to 14 per cent in 1998. In the Czech Republic, the sympathy for a strong authoritarian leader was supported by one-quarter of the Czech electorate at the beginning of transformation in 1992. Support for a non-democratic Czech dictator went down to 16 per cent in 1994 and remained at the low level of slightly more than one-tenth in 1996 and 1998. The alternative of a strong authoritarian leader is the least popular in the Czech Republic in comparison with the other Central European countries.

Within the Balkans, the wish for a strong leader, who supposedly would quickly solve the political problems of transformation, is greatest in Bulgaria and Romania. The desire for one strong politician is highest in Bulgaria, where 66 per cent asked for an authoritarian leader in 1992! This wish for a strong man in Bulgaria decreased to 45 per cent in 1994 and 22 per cent in 1996, but went up again to 29 per cent in 1998. The wish for a strong leading politician instead of democratic pluralism is constantly quite high in Romania with a range between 27 and 30 per cent of the Romanian population demanding that alternative to democracy. In the Federal Republic of Yugoslavia the wish for a strong leader is only supported by 12 per cent of the electorate. It may be the case that the experience of President Milosevic, who is definitely a strong leader, has cooled the demand for one strong man on top of the Serbian political system. The same phenomenon appears to have occurred in Croatia, where only between 5 and 11 per cent of the Croatian electorate express their wish for a strong authoritarian leader. As in Serbia-Montenegro, the longer exposure of the Croatian general public to a strong leader, President Tudjman, seems to have had the effect of almost no desire to have another strong leader in the future.

The wish of the general public for a strong authoritarian leader instead of pluralist democracy is by far the greatest in the countries in Eastern Europe, in the Ukraine, Belarus and in Russia. Throughout the whole period between 1992 and 1998, we find an absolute majority of the Ukrainian population who have a preference for a strong political leader to pluralist democracy. This wish for a one-man regime following a one-party regime was even increasing from 53 per cent in 1992 to 67 per cent in 1996. Only since 1996 has the demand for a strong politician decreased in the Ukraine somewhat to 55 per cent in 1998, which still represents an absolute majority for that alternative to democracy. This wish for a strong political leader might have had decisive consequences for the presidential elections in the Ukraine, which took place in November 1999. The support for a strong authoritarian leader was greatest at the beginning of transformation in Belarus, when 76 per cent of the Byelorussian electorate wanted such an alternative to democracy. Since 1992, that share of supporters of an one-man system decreased to 57 in 1994 and finally to 37 per cent in 1998. One explanation for that declining support for a strong leader might come from the fact that Belarus has already a strong authoritarian leader in the person of President Alexander Lukashenka and almost such a type of non-democratic regime, thus one could argue that this wish of the Byelorussian population is already ful-filled. In the Russian Federation the desire for an authoritarian ruler is somewhat smaller in comparison with Belarus and the Ukraine. Only one-third of the Russian electorate (33 per cent) were in favour of a strong Russian leader in 1994 and slightly more (36 per cent) four years later, in 1998.

Alternatives to democracy: support for a military regime

Another alternative to democracy, which is less popular than a strong authoritarian leader within post-Communist Europe, is the wish for the replacement of democracy by a military regime. That wish was measured by the question, whether the national army should govern the country (see Table 3.5). The development over time shows that support for the rule of the military is constantly low with less than 10 per cent of all post-Communist citizens and without an upwards or downwards tendency. In 1994, only 9 per cent of the population in all eleven countries favoured the political take-over by the national army, thus replacing the young democracy by military rule. This share went down slightly to 8 per cent in 1996 and up again to 9 per cent in 1998. Almost nobody in Central Europe (3 per cent) wants the army to govern the country. In Southern Europe we find a similar level of support for a military regime as in Eastern Europe: in both regions 12 per cent of the electorate are in favour of military dictatorship.

In 1994, 11 per cent of the Polish population supported military rule instead of democracy, which was maybe an outcome of positive experi-ences of military rule under President and General Wojciech Jaruzelski during the 1980s in Poland. This figure went down to 6 per cent in 1998, which is still the highest level of support for military dictatorship in the Central European buffer zone. The support for military rule in Slovakia with 6 per cent in 1998 was as high as in Poland. In the Czech Republic we find consistently 3 per cent of the Czech population who prefer a military

Table 3.5 Alternatives to democracy: support for a military regime

Q. Do you agree or disagree with the view that it is best that the army should govern the country?

Country	NDB 3 1994	NDB 4 1996	NDB 5 1998	Change 1994–8
Central Europe	5	3	3	−2
Poland	11	4	6	−5
Slovakia	4	1	6	2
Czech Republic	2	3	3	1
Slovenia	8	4	1	−7
Hungary	2	3	1	−1
Southern Europe	12	9	12	0
Romania	19	12	18	−1
Bulgaria	14	15	13	−1
FR of Yugoslavia	*	*	12	*
Croatia	3	1	4	1
Northern Europe	4	4	*	0
Lithuania	6	5	*	−1
Latvia	4	4	*	0
Estonia	3	2	*	−1
Eastern Europe	12	13	13	1
Russia	10	11	15	5
Ukraine	10	15	14	4
Belarus	15	13	10	−5

Notes
* Not done in this country at this time.
Percentage people agreeing.

regime to pluralist democracy. In Slovenia (1 per cent in 1998) and Hungary (1 per cent in 1998) virtually nobody is in favour of the army taking over power in their country and hence replacing democracy. In Slovenia, we found 8 per cent supporting military rule in 1994, but this support disappeared during the second half of the 1990s.

Within Southern Europe, the support for military rule is quite high in the two countries on the Black Sea, Bulgaria and Romania. We find the greatest desire for military rule in comparison with all post-Communist states in Romania, where between 18 and 19 per cent of the population think that the best form of a Romanian government would be a military regime. We also find between 13 and 15 per cent of the Bulgarian electorate favouring a military take-over. In the Federal Republic of Yugoslavia, 12 per cent of the population think that the best political solution for the country would be a military government. In contrast to the other Balkan countries of Romania, Bulgaria and Serbia, the population of Croatia is not in favour of a military regime in Croatia: only 4 per cent support the political leadership of the Croatian army, which is a level of support almost as low as in Slovenia.

In Eastern Europe, the support for a military regime is decisively lower than the support for a restoration of a Communist regime or a one-man dictatorship, but the patterns are divergent in those former member states of the Soviet Union. In the Russian Federation, the desire for a military regime grew over time from 10 per cent in 1994 to 15 per cent in 1998. The general dissatisfaction with the current democracy in Russia is obviously reflected in growing support for alternatives to democracy. In the Ukraine, we find a constant level of 14 per cent of the Ukrainian electorate who prefer military rule to democracy. Quite contrary to Russia, the support for a military regime in Belarus decreased from 15 per cent in 1994 to 10 per cent in 1998.

Alternatives to democracy: support for the monarchy

Many post-Communist countries have the historical experience of monarchy as a form of political regime. The research question was now, to what extent did the post-Communist citizen regard the monarchy as an alternative to a parliamentary democracy at the end of the twentieth century? The main result was that approximately one-tenth of the population in post-Communist Europe favours the monarchy as an alternative to democracy (see Table 3.6). The share of monarchists grew from 7 per cent in 1994 to 9 per cent in 1998 in post-Communist Europe. The wish for a monarchist restoration is very small in Central Europe, where consistently

Table 3.6 Alternatives to democracy: support for the monarchy

Q. Do you agree or disagree with the view that a return to a monarchy would be better?

Country	NDB 3 1994	NDB 5 1998	Change 1994–8
Central Europe	4	4	0
Slovakia	2	5	3
Poland	6	4	−2
Czech Republic	3	4	1
Hungary	5	4	−1
Slovenia	*	3	*
Southern Europe	14	14	0
FR of Yugoslavia	*	24	*
Bulgaria	19	18	−1
Romania	18	11	−7
Croatia	4	3	−1
Eastern Europe	8	10	2
Ukraine	7	12	5
Russia	9	11	2
Belarus	8	8	0

Notes
*Not done in this country at this time.
Percentage people agreeing.

only 4 per cent support monarchy as a political regime. In Eastern Europe, the support for the establishment of a new Tsar grew from 8 per cent in 1994 to 10 per cent in 1998, reflecting the general dissatisfaction with democracy in these three former Soviet Republics. In Southern Europe, the wish for the restoration of monarchy is highest in comparison with the other post-Communist regions. A constant share of 14 per cent of all Southern Europeans favour a return to monarchy.

The most advanced states in Central Europe can be described as the most republican and the least monarchist. A revival of the monarchy in Central Europe is not supported by the general public of the candidates of the first round of enlargement of the European Union. The relatively highest support for monarchy within the Central European buffer zone is found in Slovakia, where the support for monarchy went up from 2 per cent in 1994 to 5 per cent in 1998. Popular demand for a new Polish King shrank from 6 per cent in 1994 to 4 per cent in 1998. In the Czech Republic, the wish for a new monarchy went up slightly from 3 per cent in 1994 to 4 per cent in 1998. The wish for the restoration of monarchy, maybe of the House of Habsburg, decreased from 5 per cent to 4 per cent in 1998. Support for the monarchy in Slovenia is marginal: only 3 per cent of the Slovenes prefer a monarchy to the existing democracy in their country.

The greatest level of support for a return to monarchy all over post-Communist Europe was found in the Federal Republic of Yugoslavia, where 14 per cent of the population in 1998 expressed their opinion that a return to a Yugoslav monarchy would be better. In Bulgaria, approximately one-fifth of the population – between 18 and 19 per cent – consistently think in a positive way about the restoration of the Bulgarian dynasty. The desire for the restoration of the Romanian dynasty cooled from 18 per cent in 1994 to 11 per cent in 1998, but is still considerably high. In Croatia we find again by analogy to Slovenia almost no support (3 per cent) for the restoration of monarchy.

Within Eastern Europe, the general and persisting crisis of the political systems is boosting the wish for the return of the Tsar or the king along other dynastical and historical lines. The wish for a return to monarchy is highest in the Ukraine and increased from 7 per cent in 1994 to 12 per cent in 1998, again indicating the deep dissatisfaction of the Ukrainian general public with the current democratic regime. The desire for the return of the Romanovs in Russia is growing from 9 per cent in 1994 to 11 per cent in 1998. More than one in ten Russian citizens prefer a Tsarist regime to the current Russian democracy. In Belarus, we find a constant group of 8 per cent of the Byelorussian electorate who are convinced that a return to monarchy would be better than the current regime in Belarus.

Measuring democracy: a new index of democracy

On the basis of the analysis of new democracies in Chapters 2 and 3, I developed an 'index of democracy' at the level of the post-Communist general publics (see Table 3.7). The aim of the index is to measure the extent of individual level democratisation of societies in transformation from non-democratic to democratic regimes. The index of democratisation aims at identifying those segments of post-Communist societies which we can rightly label as 'democrats' or 'democratic citizens', people who identify with the concept of pluralistic democracy, without necessarily supporting the political regime of the day, which could be democratic to a greater or lesser extent or non-democratic to a greater or lesser extent. The index of democracy, which is presented in this book for the very first time, does not measure the rating of the performance of the current government at a given point in time; it is supposed to measure the support for democracy as a principle and a form of regime, as opposed to other, non-democratic forms of political regime.

The index of democracy consists of nine different items, most of which have been already described in Chapter 2 and some in Chapter 3 in more detail.

Index of democracy: a nine-item index

Item 1: Negative rating of Communist political regime in the past (cf. Chapter 2).
Question: Here is a scale for ranking how the system of government works. The top, +100, is the best; the bottom, −100, the worst. Where on this scale would you put the former Communist regime?

Included in that item as 'democratic' are all people who give the old Communist political regime a negative evaluation between −10 and −100.

Item 2: Positive rating of New Democracy or current political regime (cf. Chapter 3).
Question: Here is a scale for ranking how the system of government works. The top, +100, is the best; the bottom, −100, the worst. Where on this scale would you put the current system of governing with free elections and many parties?

Included in that item as 'democratic' are all people who give the current new democracy a positive evaluation between +10 and +100.

Item 3: Optimism about the future of democratic parliaments (cf. Chapter 3).
Question: Some people think this country would be better governed if parliament were closed down and all parties were abolished. How likely do you think this is to happen in the next few years?

Included in that item as 'democratic' are all people who assume that the closure of the democratic parliament and abolition of all democratic parties are 'not very likely' or 'not at all likely'.

Item 4: Support for democratic national parliament (cf. Chapter 3).
Question: Some people think this country would be better governed if parliament were closed down and all parties were abolished. Would you approve or disapprove?

Included in that item as 'democratic' are all people who would 'definitely disapprove' or 'somewhat disapprove' if parliament were closed down and the democratic parties were abolished.

Item 5: Rejection of authoritarian leader as alternative to democracy (cf. Chapter 3).
Question: Our present system of government is not the only one this country has had. Some people say that we would be better off if the country was governed differently. What do you think? Please tell me whether you agree or disagree with the statement that it would be best to get rid of parliament and elections and to have a strong leader who can quickly decide everything.

Included in that item as 'democratic' are all people who 'strongly disagree' or 'somewhat disagree' with a strong leader as alternative to democracy.

Item 6: Rejection of a military regime as alternative to democracy (cf. Chapter 3).
Question: Our present system of government is not the only one this country has had. Some people say that we would be better off if the country was governed differently. What do you think? Please tell me whether you agree or disagree with the statement that it would be best if the army governs the country.

Included in that item as 'democratic' are all people who 'strongly disagree' or 'somewhat disagree' with a military regime as alternative to democracy.

Item 7: Rejection of the monarchy as an alternative to democracy (cf. Chapter 3).
Question: Our present system of government is not the only one this country has had. Some people say that we would be better off if the country was governed differently. What do you think? Please tell me whether you agree or disagree with the statement that a return to a monarchy would be better.

Included in that item as 'democratic' are all people who 'strongly disagree' or 'somewhat disagree' with a return or new establishment of a monarchy as alternative to democracy. In the three Baltic countries, this question was not asked. As functional equivalent we used the following question: If our system (of democracy) cannot produce results soon, that's a good reason to try some other system of government? Included in that item as 'democratic' are all people in the three Baltic states who reject this statement and display political patience with the new democratic political system. From this point of view, the index of democracy is strictly comparable in all analysed post-Communist countries except the three Baltic countries.

Item 8: Rejection of return to Communist political regime as alternative to democracy (cf. Chapter 2).
Question: Our present system of government is not the only one this country has had. Some people say that we would be better off if the country was governed differently. What do you think? Please tell me whether you agree or disagree with the statement that it would be best that we should return to Communist rule.

Included in that item as 'democratic' are all people who 'strongly disagree' or 'somewhat disagree' with a return to Communist rule as alternative to democracy.

Item 9: Optimism about the future of democracy
Question: Here is a scale for ranking how the system of government works. The top, +100, is the best, the bottom, −100, the worst.

> Where on this scale would you put our system of governing with free elections and many parties five years in the future?
>
> Included in that item as 'democratic' are all people who give the future democracy a positive evaluation between +10 and +100.

The index of democracy consists finally of 10 values. Value 10 means, for example, that a person is 'democratic' on all 9 items, value 9 means that a respondent is democratic on 8 out of 9 items, value 1 means that a person is 'non-democratic' on all 9 items.

The resulting groups are defined as follows:

A	democrats	values 9–10
B	weak democrats	value 8
C	weak non-democrats	value 7
D	non-democrats	values 1–6

Only those persons are included in the index of democracy who are democratic on either 7 out of 9 items, 8 out of 9 items or on all 9 items, which ensures a very strict operationalisation of 'democrats'. The index of democracy encompasses the category of 'democrats' (= values 9–10) as well as the group of 'weak democrats' (= value 8). The results are shown in Table 3.7.

If, in a given society, more than 60 per cent of the population can be labelled as 'democrats', then I am talking about a 'consolidated democracy'. This notion of consolidated democracy refers to the individual level of the post-Communist citizen. The process of consolidation of democracy at the meso level and at the macro level has to be measured with other methods. The extent of democratisation at the level of elites and of institutions is to be analysed with other political science research methods. We are focusing here at the extent of democracy at the micro-level of transforming societies. If, in a given society, more than 40 per cent of the electorate are identified as 'democrats', then we can talk of emerging democracies. All societies with a share of less than 40 per cent democrats are transforming societies, where democracy is one path of political development among a variety of regime forms, and the outcome of transformation in those societies is uncertain and does not lead inevitably towards democracy.

The analysis of this newly created index of democracy clearly shows the different degrees of democratisation in post-Communist Europe. In Central Europe an average of 61 per cent of the general public can be

Table 3.7 Index of democracy in post-Communist societies

Country	NDB 3 1994	NDB 4 1996	NDB 5 1998	Change 1994–8
Central Europe mean	57	52	61	4
Poland	47	52	66	19
Czech Republic	77	69	65	−12
Hungary	50	38	62	12
Slovenia	*	47	57	10
Slovakia	55	53	55	0
Southern Europe mean	56	52	55	−1
Romania	59	60	56	−3
Croatia	65	51	55	−10
Bulgaria	44	45	54	10
FR of Yugoslavia	*	*	37	*
Northern Europe mean	28	30	*	2
Estonia	43	46	*	3
Lithuania	18	27	*	9
Latvia	22	18	*	−4
Eastern Europe mean	21	14	30	9
Belarus	23	15	41	18
Ukraine	25	12	19	−6
Russia	15	*	*	*

Sources: NDB 3 (1994), NDB 4 (1996), NDB 5 (1998), New Baltic Barometer 1994, New Baltic Barometer 1996.

Notes
*Not done in this country at this time.
Index of democracy, values 8–10.

described as 'democrats'. One therefore can confirm the hypothesis that the countries of the Central European region are already consolidated democracies regarding their citizens. The country with the most 'democrats' is Poland: in 1998, 66 per cent of all Polish citizens are 'democrats'. In 1994, we find only 47 per cent democrats in the Polish electorate, which increased to 52 per cent of democratic Polish citizens in 1996. The change from an emerging to a consolidated democracy in Poland occurred between 1996 and 1998. Since 1998, Poland has certainly been a member of the group of European consolidated democracies and is therefore well prepared for political European integration at the level of the European general publics. The Czech Republic, where 65 per cent of the Czech electorate are democratic citizens in 1998, fills the second rank regarding the level of democratisation. The Czech trend was opposite to the Polish trend: in 1994, 77 per cent of the Czech population had democratic attitudes, almost a 'euphoria' for democracy, the political events and their popular perception during the governments under Prime Ministers Vaclav Klaus and Milos Zeman were a cold shower for the 'euphoria for democracy' and for the role of the Czech Republic as a self-ascribed 'ideal-type of democratic transformation'. Nevertheless, it is justified to label the current Czech political system a consolidated democracy in the same league as Poland. Also quite high is the share of democratic citizens in Hungary with 62 per cent 'democrats' in 1998. In the first years of political transformation we witnessed a high degree of scepticism about democracy in general and the new Hungarian democracy in particular, there were only 38 per cent democrats in 1996, but in 1998 the Hungarian general public supported the new democracy with more than 60 per cent, which puts Hungary clearly in the first group of consolidated democracies in Central and Eastern Europe together with Poland and the Czech Republic. After ten years of political transformation, three out of fifteen post-Communist countries have reached the status of a consolidated democracy: Poland, the Czech Republic and Hungary. In Slovenia, my analysis identified a share of 57 per cent of democratic citizens, which puts the Slovenian democracy just below the threshold of 60 per cent for qualifying as a consolidated democracy. It can be assumed that Slovenia will have reached the status of such a democracy at the beginning of the new century. In Slovakia, we have a constant majority of well above 50 per cent of the Slovak electorate, which can be labelled democrats. In 1998, an absolute majority of Slovak citizens of 55 per cent have democratic values and attitudes. The proof of this occurred at the general elections in autumn 1998, when the government of Prime Minister Dzurinda replaced the government of Prime Minister Meciar. Within the whole region of central Europe, I did not find any new political system, where less than 50 per cent of the electorate consisted of democratic citizens, embracing the principles and values of pluralistic democracy and constituting the general public support for democracy in the future.

In Southern Europe, we find a majority for democracy in almost all countries of that troubled region. The average share of democratic citizens in Southern Europe is 55 per cent. However, there are no consolidated democracies yet found in Southern Europe. In countries like Romania, Croatia and Bulgaria, we find an absolute majority of democratic citizens well above 50 per cent, but currently the threshold for consolidated democracies has not been reached by any Southern European country. Romania comes closest to a consolidated democracy with 56 per cent of democratic Romanians, but still needs an increase of between 5 and 10 per cent more democratic citizens in order to qualify as a consolidated democracy. In Croatia, we find a special situation with 65 per cent of democratic citizens in 1994: at this early stage of political transformation, the Croatian general electorate was heavily influenced by two political factors: Croatia was a country at war with its neighbours and was also a newly independent state. Both factors distorted and biased the survey results in Croatia towards some sort of wartime enthusiasm for one's own and new besieged country. The case of Bulgaria is quite interesting. The share of Bulgarian democrats gradually increased from 44 per cent in 1994 to 54 per cent in 1998, despite enormous political and economic difficulties in the first phase of transformation, especially due to the deadlock during the first post-Communist government by the Bulgarian Socialist Party (BSP), the successor party to the Bulgarian Communist Party. Within the Southern European region, the three main countries – Romania, Croatia and Bulgaria – can all be described as emerging democracies with a share of around 55 per cent of their respective general publics, which I label 'democrats'. The interesting dilemma here is that the process of democratisation is well under way at the individual level of the post-Communist citizen, whereas the democratisation at the meso-level and at the macro-level of the political systems, in terms of, for example, the building of democratic institutions and the formation of democratic elites, is lagging somewhat behind. In the Federal Republic of Yugoslavia, I did find, despite the authoritarian regime of President Milosevic and the fact that Serbia and Montenegro are societies that have been at war for many years, a group of 37 per cent of the Yugoslav general public who have democratic principles and attitudes. That group seems to be the core group for democratic change of the Federal Republic of Yugoslavia in the future.

In the Baltic States, no consolidated democracy could be found. Only Estonia qualified as an emerging democracy with a share of democratic Estonians of 46 per cent in 1996. In Lithuania, there are only 27 per cent 'democrats' in 1996, whereas in Latvia, I could identity even less democratic citizens, namely 18 per cent. The extent of individual-level democratisation in Northern post-Communist Europe is more similar to the post-Soviet patterns in Eastern Europe than to the paths of transition in Central Europe. In Eastern Europe, an average of 30 per cent of post-Soviet citizens can be described as 'democrats'. The highest share of democratic citizens was found in Belarus with 41 per cent democratic citizens in 1998. In the Ukraine, only 19 per cent support the principles and values of parliamentary democracy in 1998; in Russia, the share of democratic citizens is by far the lowest: only 15 per cent of the Russian electorate qualify as 'democrats' according to my definition in 1994. In Eastern Europe, we could not find any consolidated democracy at the individual level, which was not much of a surprise and only Belarus has more than 40 per cent of the electorate with democratic attitudes, which was some surprise, considering the gap between democratisation at the level of the general public and the state of the political system in Belarus, but which could be an indication of some democratic pressures from below against the current authoritarian regime of President Lukashenka.

4 Social structure and democracy

The impact of education upon support for democracy

The core social group of 'democrats' in post-Communist societies are people with tertiary education throughout the whole region. In Central Europe, on average 79 per cent of all post-Communist citizens with academic degrees or students support democracy as a form of government and thus are the backbone of democracy. The share of democrats within the highest level of education in Central European countries grew from 74 per cent in 1994 to 79 per cent in 1998 (see Table 4.1). The highest number of democrats within the tertiary level of education was found in

Table 4.1 Percentage of democrats within the group of persons with tertiary education

Country	1994	1996	1998	Change 1994–8
Central Europe mean	74	76	79	5
Hungary	76	65	88	12
Poland	65	75	86	21
Czech Republic	95	88	80	−15
Slovakia	58	72	72	14
Slovenia	*	80	71	−9
Southern Europe	67	60	62	−5
Romania	79	69	77	−2
Bulgaria	61	60	74	13
Croatia	62	50	56	−6
FR of Yugoslavia	*	*	41	*
Northern Europe	42	44	*	2
Estonia	60	62	*	2
Lithuania	38	40	*	2
Latvia	27	29	*	2
Eastern Europe mean	31	20	37	6
Belarus	32	21	47	15
Ukraine	36	19	26	−10
Russia	25	*	*	*

Note
* Not done in this country at this time.

Hungary, where 88 per cent of all Hungarian graduates and students support democracy in a definite manner. The democratisation of the Hungarian graduates can be derived from the fact that we found 76 per cent of democrats in that social group in 1994 and that this share went up to 88 per cent in 1998. The expansion of democratic support was most visible in Polish society: in 1994, only 65 per cent of all Polish graduates supported the young Polish democracy, whereas in 1998 the share of democrats in the highest Polish educational group went up steeply to 86 per cent. The pattern in the Czech Republic was quite different to the pattern in Hungary and Poland. An amazing 95 per cent of all Czech graduates supported democracy in 1994; the observation of the reality of Czech democracy and some form of sobering up after the democratic euphoria in the first half of the 1990s reduced the share of democrats in the tertiary educational group to 80 per cent in 1998 (Haerpfer and Wallace 1998). The process of democratisation of Slovak society was much slower than in Hungary, Poland and the Czech Republic and happened at a somewhat lower level. In 1994, only 58 per cent of Slovaks with higher education were in favour of democracy as a new form of political regime; this share of democrats increased to 72 per cent in 1998 at the end of the era of Prime Minister Meciar. In Slovenia we find, in a similar way as in the Czech Republic, a shift from democratic euphoria to realism: in 1998, only 71 per cent of those with a tertiary level of education in Slovenia support democracy, which puts Slovenia in the same group as Slovakia, well behind Hungary, Poland and the Czech Republic as well. The Hungarians and Poles with tertiary education can be described as 'mature democrats' with a share close to 90 per cent. The graduates and students in the Czech Republic, Slovakia and Slovenia easily fulfil the criterion of citizens in a 'consolidating democracy' (= range between 60 and 80 per cent of democrats) with values between 70 and 80 per cent, the Czechs being on the threshold of a 'mature democracy'.

The extent of democratisation of higher educated people in Southern Europe is significantly lower than in Central Europe: only 67 per cent of the Southern European graduates and students were democrats in 1994, a mean share, which shrank to 62 per cent in 1998. Within Southern Europe, we are able to identify two different patterns of democratisation, one specific in Southern countries on the Black Sea and another in the former Yugoslavia. In Romania and Bulgaria, the highest educational stratum fulfils the criterion of a consolidating democracy with a share of democrats well above 70 per cent. In Romania, the percentage of democrats among Romanian graduates went down slightly from 79 per cent in 1994 to 77 per cent in 1998. The high value in 1994 was maybe due to the enormous relief of the Romanian public at the end of the old non-democratic regime in Romania. In Bulgaria, on the other hand, we can speak of a stable rise of democratic attitudes and values within the tertiary level of education from a share of 61 per cent in 1994 up to 74 per cent in 1998.

The extent of democratisation among graduates is very similar in Bulgaria and in Romania, both countries can be labelled consolidating democracies with regard to certain social groups, at least as far as the graduates and students are concerned. The picture is quite different in Croatia and Serbia-Montenegro: in Croatia, the share of democrats within the group of graduates and university students decreased from 62 per cent in 1994 to 56 per cent in 1998. In the Federal Republic of Yugoslavia, only 41 per cent of citizens with tertiary education support democracy. This low level of democratisation of the highly educated in Croatia and Serbia-Montenegro is possibly due to the fact that the authoritarian regimes of Presidents Milosevic and Tudjman and the experience of regional military conflicts made it very difficult for the general public in these post-Yugoslav successor states to develop democratic values and a democratic political culture. The Croatian highly educated citizens fulfil the criterion of an emerging democracy (= values between 40 and 60 per cent of democrats); the Serbian graduates are just above the threshold for a consolidating democracy.

In the Baltic States, the level of democratisation within the group of graduates is much lower than in Central Europe and in Southern Europe. Only 42 per cent of Baltic citizens within the tertiary group of education were democrats in 1994, which increased slightly to 44 per cent in 1996. A clear-cut majority for democracy is found in Estonia, where 62 per cent of the Estonian graduates and students are identified as democrats. The share of highly educated democrats is, at 40 per cent, much lower in Lithuania than in Estonia. In Latvia, finally, we find the lowest level of democratisation among the Baltic States, only 29 per cent of the highly educated Latvians can be described as democrats.

In Eastern Europe, the number of highly educated democrats increased from 31 per cent in 1994 to 37 per cent in 1998. Surprisingly, we find a shift of democratisation at the level of the general public in Belarus. In 1994, only 32 per cent of graduates and students could be labelled democrats; this share went up to 47 per cent in 1998, despite the non-democratic regime of President Lukashenka in the same period. Thus, Belarus seems to be the interesting case of a society becoming more democratic, when simultaneously the government of the same country becomes less democratic. The trend is exactly opposite in the Ukraine, where we find a share of 36 per cent democrats in 1994, which decreased to 26 per cent in 1998. In the period under observation, the Byelorussian electorate became more democratic and the Ukrainian society less democratic. In Russia, only a minority of 25 per cent of the highly educated Russians can be characterised as democratic.

The impact of the urban–rural dimension upon support for democracy

This section analyses the relationship between the urban–rural divide and the dynamics of democratisation in post-Communist societies. In all fifteen countries we find the same pattern that the greatest share of democrats can be found in cities and not in small villages in the countryside. In Central Europe, we find the biggest share of democrats in large cities with more than 100,000 inhabitants. This core group of 'urban democrats' in the Central European buffer zone grew from 66 per cent in 1994 to 72 per cent in 1998 (see Table 4.2). In the Czech Republic, an astonishing majority of 84 per cent of the Czech population, living in large Czech cities with more than 100,000 inhabitants, are democrats according to our definition and form the decisive core element of Czech democracy at the micro-level of the Czech citizenry. Whereas the democratic standing of Czech cities is stable over time, we do find a strong wave of democratisation in large Polish towns during the period of observation: in 1994, only 50 per cent of Poles living in large cities with more than 100,000 inhabitants were democrats. That rather lower share, if compared with Czech or Slovak large cities, increased within four years to 74 per cent of Polish urban dwellers in 1998. In Slovakia, the inhabitants of large towns like Bratislava were a democratic stronghold throughout the 1990s and the main element of

Table 4.2 Urban–rural dimension and democracy: large cities with more than 100,000 inhabitants

Country	1994	1996	1998	Change 1994–8
Central Europe mean	66	64	72	6
Czech Republic	84	84	*	0
Poland	50	58	74	24
Slovakia	74	68	73	−1
Hungary	57	57	72	15
Slovenia	*	55	70	15
Southern Europe	63	58	56	−7
Bulgaria	54	53	66	12
Romania	63	64	61 (2)	−2
Croatia	71	58	56 (2)	−15
FR of Yugoslavia	*	*	40 (2)	*
Northern Europe	31	32	*	1
Estonia	45	47	*	2
Lithuania	26	34	*	8
Latvia	23	16	*	−7
Eastern Europe	23	18	34	11
Belarus	28	22	42	14
Ukraine	23 (2)	13	26	3
Russia	18	*	*	*

Note
* Not done in this country at this time.

democratic opposition against the political regime of President Meciar. The share of democrats in large Slovak cities with more than 100,000 inhabitants is constantly around 70 per cent between 1994 and 1998. In Hungary, the relationship between urbanisation and democratisation is quite similar to the Polish case. In 1994, only 57 per cent of the Hungarians living in large towns can be described as democrats, a figure which rises to 72 per cent in 1998. In Slovenia, too, we find a wave of democratisation of large towns with an increase from 55 per cent in 1996 to 70 per cent in 1998. The general pattern in Central Europe is that the bigger cities are a stronghold of democrats and that the share of democratic urban citizens is around 70 per cent in all Central European cities, showing a high degree of democratic homogeneity in that most advanced part of post-Communist Europe. The inhabitants of major cities in the Czech Republic, Poland, Slovakia, Hungary and Slovenia easily fulfil the criteria for a consolidating democracy.

Throughout the Balkan region, the general pattern appears to be quite different. First of all, the number of democrats in larger cities decreased from 63 per cent in 1994 to 56 per cent in 1998. Second, in Romania, Croatia and Serbia, the biggest number of democrats is not found in the large cities, but in medium-sized towns of between 10,000 and 100,000 inhabitants. Only Bulgaria shows the same pattern of interactions between urbanisation and democratisation as in Central Europe. In 1994, 54 per cent of Bulgarians living in major cities like Sofia are democrats according to our definition, which increases over time to 66 per cent of democrats in large Bulgarian cities in 1998. In Romania, the strongholds of democracy were the larger Romanian cities in 1994 and 1996 with more than 60 per cent of urban democrats. Surprisingly, we find more democrats in Romanian medium-sized towns of between 10,000 and 100,000 inhabitants than in large cities in 1998. The same phenomenon occurs in Croatia: the share of democrats in large Croatian towns is shrinking between 1994 and 1996 from 71 to 58 per cent and we find a stronghold for democracy in medium-sized Croatian towns in 1998. In Serbia-Montenegro, the largest share of democrats was identified not in big cities, but in medium-sized towns of between 10,000 and 100,000 inhabitants.

In the Baltic region, the inhabitants of bigger cities can be labelled the core group of democrats, albeit at a much lower level than in Central Europe. On average, one-third of Baltic citizens, living in cities with more than 100,000 inhabitants, are democrats according to our definition. Only the urban citizens in Estonia fulfil the criterion for an emerging democracy, the inhabitants of large cities in Lithuania and Latvia fall into the category for a transforming democracy with especially low shares of democrats in Latvian towns.

The relationship between urbanisation and democratisation is in Eastern Europe at a similar level as in Northern Europe, but the longitudinal pattern is different. The share of democrats in major cities in Russia,

Belarus or the Ukraine increased from 23 per cent in 1994 to 34 per cent in 1998, which is still a minority, but a growing minority. The large cities in Belarus like Minsk became more democratic during the process of political transition. In 1994, only 23 per cent of Byelorussians living in major cities were democrats. That share almost doubled to 42 per cent democrats in 1998. In 1994, the relative strongholds of democracy along the urban–rural dimension were medium-sized towns of between 10,000 and 100,000 inhabitants with a share of 23 per cent. After a disastrous share of 13 per cent democrats in main Ukrainian cities in 1996, we can see in 1998 a low recovery of democracy at the micro-level with a share of 26 per cent democrats living in large Ukrainian cities like Kiev or L'viv.

The impact of age upon support for democracy

One crucial factor for a successful process of democratisation is the question of the support for democracy in different age groups. Our theoretical assumption is that the deeper embedded a new democracy is within the first post-Communist generation, the higher the chances of a successful and sustained democratisation of a post-totalitarian society. The older generation has spent between fifty and seventy years under Communism and the chances are very small of them transforming into democratic citizens after, say, fifty years of socialisation in a non-democratic regime on a large scale within these age cohorts.

The overall result of our analysis is that the youngest age group between 16 and 29 years of age is the most democratic age group in twelve out of fifteen post-Communist countries. Only in Poland, Slovakia and Croatia is the age group between 30 and 59 years slightly more democratic than the Polish, Slovak and Croatian youth. In Central Europe, the first post-Communist generation is the most democratic age group and they become more democratic over time. In 1994, 61 per cent of all young people in Central Europe can be defined as democrats and they are growing to 65 per cent in 1998 (see Table 4.3). The Hungarian youth is the most democratic in the post-Communist world: in 1994, only 55 per cent of the young Hungarians were democrats, their share increased to 73 per cent of all young people in Hungary in 1998. In the Czech Republic, the young generation was consistently very democratic throughout the process of transition, the percentage of young Czech democrats decreased from 78 per cent in 1994 to 70 per cent in 1998, thus reflecting the general growing realism with democracy after the democratic euphoria during the first years of transition, which had its peak in 1996. In Slovenia, the young Slovenes were also a stronghold of democracy, displaying patterns similar to Hungary and the Czech Republic. In 1996, 54 of all young Slovenes are democrats, that share increased to 61 per cent in 1998. The age distribution of democrats appears to be quite different in Poland and Slovakia, compared with the dominance of the first post-Communist

Table 4.3 Age and democracy: age group between 18 and 29 years

Country	1994	1996	1998	Change 1994–8
Central Europe mean	61	56	65	4
Hungary	55	43	73	18
Czech Republic	78	79	70	−8
Poland	54	53 (2)	68 (2)	14
Slovenia	*	54	61	7
Slovakia	56	53	55 (2)	−1
Southern Europe	60	57	57	−3
Bulgaria	55	57	71	16
Romania	62 (2)	62	64	2
Croatia	63 (2)	53	55 (2)	−8
FR of Yugoslavia	*	*	39	*
Northern Europe	31	35	*	4
Estonia	43	50	*	7
Lithuania	22	29 (2)	*	7
Latvia	28	25	*	−3
Eastern Europe	30	19	38	8
Belarus	28	20	49	21
Ukraine	32	18	26	−6
Russia	18	*	*	*

Note
* Not done in this country at this time.

generation in Hungary, the Czech Republic and Slovenia. In Poland, the most democratic age group are Polish citizens between 30 and 59 years of age and not the Polish youth. The young Polish people are also quite democratic, but their internal share of democrats is slightly lower than the percentage of democrats in the middle-aged group. In 1996, 53 per cent of the middle Polish generation can be described as democrats, a share which went up to 61 per cent in 1998. One possible explanation for that deviant pattern could be the earlier process of democratisation, which is closely connected to the activities of the Solidarity movement in Poland and resulted in a high political mobilisation of that age cohort towards democracy. In Slovakia, the young generation was the most democratic age group in 1994 (56 per cent democrats) and 1996 (53 per cent democrats), but in 1998 the middle generation of Slovaks between 30 and 59 years of age became the most democratic age group.

In Southern Europe, the pattern of the relationships between age and democracy are similar and different, if compared with Central Europe. In Southern Europe as well as in Central Europe, in most countries the young post-Communist generation is the most democratic age group. Whereas in Central Europe the size of democrats within the post-Communist generation grew during transition, it is rather stable at a very high level in Southern Europe. In 1994, 60 per cent of young Southern Europeans were democrats; this figure went down slightly to 57 per cent in 1998. Again the pattern in Bulgaria is very close to the pattern in

Central Europe in general, to the situation in Hungary in particular in that case. In 1994, an absolute majority of 55 per cent of young Bulgarians are democrats, which increased to 71 per cent in 1998. In Romania, an absolute majority of 64 per cent of young Romanians can be described as democrats. Hence, the first post-Communist generations in Bulgaria and Romania fulfil the criterion for consolidating democracies with a share of democrats between 60 and 80 per cent. The age group with the greatest share of democrats in Serbia-Montenegro are young people under 29 years. Within the first post-Communist generation in Serbia, 39 per cent are democrats according to our definition, still a minority, even among the Serbian youth. The influence of age upon democracy is again different in Croatia, where the middle generation is the most democratic age group like in Poland and Slovakia. An absolute majority of 55 per cent of Croats between 30 and 59 years are democrats and the stronghold of democracy in the era of President Tudjman, in 1998.

The Baltic youth is the core group of democracy, albeit at a much lower level than the young people in Central Europe or Southern Europe. In 1994, 31 per cent of young citizens in the three Baltic States were democrats, a share which increased to 35 per cent in 1996. We find the strongest support for democracy in Estonia, where 50 per cent of the young generation can be described as democratic. In Latvia, only 25 per cent of the young Latvians are democrats with a declining tendency. In Lithuania, finally, we find the Polish pattern that the middle generation of Lithuanians between 30 and 59 years of age are the core group of democracy and not the Lithuanian youth.

Surprisingly, support for democracy of the Eastern European youth is, on average, higher than among the Baltic youth. In 1994, 30 per cent of the post-Soviet youth were democrats, which increased to 38 per cent in 1998. The most dynamic is that process of democratisation within the young post-Soviet generation in Belarus, where the share of democrats went up from 28 per cent in 1994 to 49 per cent in 1998, reaching the level of Estonia and clearly overtaking the Serbian youth in terms of democratic mindedness. In the Ukraine, the percentage of democratic young people went down from 32 per cent in 1994 to 26 per cent in 1998, thus reflecting the shrinking overall support for democracy in the Ukraine. In the Russian Federation, finally, only a depressing share of 18 per cent of young Russian can be defined as democrats.

The impact of gender upon support for democracy

The general outcome of the analysis of the relationship between gender and democracy for that period of transformations is that in general we do find a greater share of democrats among men than among women. In Central Europe, there are consistently 5 per cent more male democrats than female democrats throughout the period of observation. In Slovakia we find – against the general trend – a slightly bigger group of female democrats in 1994 and 1996, but in 1998 the group of male democrats is 9 per cent greater than their female counterpart (see Table 4.4). In Slovenia, the gender gap is 8 per cent in favour for Slovene men, almost as big as in Slovakia. In Poland the male dominance is shrinking over time from 11 per cent in 1994 to 4 per cent in 1998. In the Czech Republic and Hungary there is almost no difference between men and women with regard to the extent of democratisation within both social groups. The gender gap in favour of Czech men is 3 per cent; in Hungary we find even more democratic women than men, making Hungary the only Central European country with more democratic women than men.

In the Balkans, the gender gap in favour of democratic men is somewhat bigger than in Central Europe. Within the group of Southern European men we find 5 per cent more male democrats than female democrats in 1994; this share went up to 6 per cent in 1998. The advantage of democratic men over democratic women is clear-cut in Romania with a gap of 5 per cent in 1994, which grew to 10 per cent in 1998. In Croatia as well as in Serbia-Montenegro, we find 6 per cent more men than women in the group of democrats. That share is rather stable in Croatia. In Bulgaria, however, the gender gap in favour of men was melting from 5 per cent in 1994 to 3 per cent in 1998. An interesting

Table 4.4 Gender and democracy

Country	1994 Male–Female	1996 Male–Female	1998 Male–Female	Change 1994–8
Central Europe mean	5	5	5	0
Slovakia	−0.3	−1.3	9	9
Slovenia	4	16	8	4
Poland	11	−0.5	4	−7
Czech Republic	4	−0.5	3	−1
Hungary	7	9	0.5	−8
Southern Europe	5	7	6	1
Romania	5	9	10	5
Croatia	5	7	6	1
FR of Yugoslavia	*	*	6	*
Bulgaria	5	5	3	−2
Northern Europe	4	4	*	0
Estonia	5	6	*	1
Lithuania	1	5	*	4
Latvia	7	−0.2	*	−7
Eastern Europe	5	5	5	0
Russia	6	*	*	*
Ukraine	8	3	6	−2
Belarus	2	6	−0.6	−2

Note
* Not done in this country at this time.

phenomenon seems to be that in the countries of the former Yugoslavia many more men are democrats then women; this is the case not only in Serbia-Montenegro and Croatia, but also in Slovenia. In the most advanced democracies in post-Communist Europe, in Hungary, the Czech Republic and Poland, the gender gap is either very small or nil. A higher level of democratisation at the level of the general public seems to imply a convergence of democrats across the borders of gender and an increasing similarity of the sexes in that crucial dimension of a successful political transformation.

In Northern Europe we find that the male Baltic citizens are more democratic than the female Baltic citizens, especially in Estonia and Lithuania. In both Baltic countries the gender gap in favour of men is about 5 per cent. In Latvia, on the other hand, we do not find differences related to gender in the analysis of Latvian democrats. The Baltic pattern is very similar to the pattern in Eastern Europe. In Russia and the Ukraine, more men are democratic than post-Soviet women, with a gender gap of 6 per cent. The same gender gap of 6 per cent could be found in 1996 in Belarus, but the strong wave of democratisation of the Byelorussian electorate between 1996 and 1998 resulted in an equal share of male and female democrats in Belarus. This democratisation of the Byelorussian general public at the micro-level must not be mistaken for a democratisation at the macro-level of government, which did not take place at all (Marples 1999).

The relationship of social structure and democracy

Finally, all elements of social structure, which have been discussed, are integrated in a multivariate model, which analyses the impact of socio-demographic factors upon support for democracy in post-Communist Europe (see Table 4.5). The overall result of this multivariate statistic is that socio-economic phenomena such as education, age or gender explain only 4 per cent of the variance regarding the democratisation of the

Table 4.5 Social structure and democracy

	1994	*1996*	*1998*	*Change*
Education	+0.10	+0.14	+0.13	+0.03
Age	−0.07	−0.10	−0.08	−0.01
Gender – men	+0.07	+0.09	+0.05	−0.02
Religiosity	−0.11	−0.07	−0.06	+0.05
Town size	+0.08	+0.04	+0.05	−0.03
R^2	0.04	0.05	0.04	0
Significance	0.00	0.00	0.00	0

Note
OLS-regression: figures are beta-coefficients.

general publics in post-Communist Europe. The level explained variance remained constant at around 4 per cent between 1994 and 1998. Hence, we can postulate that the explanatory power of variables of social structure is quite low compared to other dimensions explaining the complex processes of democratisation in post-Communist societies.

We have been able to identify five significant influences of social structure upon democracy in Central and Eastern Europe: education, age, gender, religiosity and the urban–rural dimension. The hierarchy of influences upon democratisation is quite clear. The most important influence of social structure on the democratic development at the level of the national electorates happens to be education with a regression coefficient of 0.13. The impact of education upon democracy is growing during the process of political transformation from 0.10 (= beta) in 1994 to 0.13 (= beta) in 1998. Hence, the important link between post-Communist citizens with tertiary education and democracy has been strengthened over time.

The second most important influence of social structure upon democracy is age: the younger the citizen, the more democratic the basic political orientation. The impact of age was −0.07 in 1994; it increased to −0.10 in 1996 and it is still −0.08 in 1998. The association between the young Central and Eastern Europeans with their new democracy is quite strong and persistent over time. The third place in the hierarchy of sociodemographic influences is occupied by gender. Throughout Central and Eastern Europe men are somewhat more democratic than women, but this male lead in the process of democratisation of post-Communist publics is shrinking over time from +0.07 in 1994 to +0.05 in 1998. In fourth position we found religiosity: the impact of religiosity is negative, which means that less religiosity is correlated with higher support for democracy. The revival of religions and of associated religiosity in the form of churchgoing after the end of Communism does not inevitably imply more support for democracy. It is possible and plausible to be religious, say, a Catholic in Poland or a supporter of the Orthodox Church in Russia, without necessarily being a democrat. In a longitudinal perspective the association between democratisation on the one hand and not being religious is weakened from −0.11 in 1994 to −0.06 in 1998. The influence with the smallest impact upon democracy in the realm of a given social structure is the urban–rural dimension, measured by the size of community. The impact of town size was, with a beta coefficient of +0.08, comparatively high in 1994, but the difference between post-Communist citizens on the countryside and in cities decreased to +0.05 in 1998. Nevertheless, we still find in most post-Communist countries the strongholds of democracy more in towns than in villages.

5 Economic well-being of households and democracy

The impact of economic transformation from planned economy to market economy upon households: winners and losers

The literature on economic transformation very often refers to macro-economic indicators such as GDP per capita, economic growth rates and so on in order to measure the success or failure of economic reforms. Our research on political, economic and social transformations in Central and Eastern Europe since 1989 goes beyond that analysis at the macro-level, which is necessary, but by no means sufficient to describe the political, social and economic revolutions in Europe since the demise of Communism, let alone explain them. The collapse of the planned economy and the lack of new economic institutions at the very beginning of economic transition put all households under enormous pressure at the micro-levels, because all the stabilities of the old economic system disappeared and left the households without basic reliable expectations about the immediate future. The households and their members were suddenly forced to rethink their portfolio of economic activities with the central goal of surviving financially and economically in the first stage of economic transformation. The crucial research question in that context was, which households were able to cope economically with the rapid economic change and which households had difficulties in adapting to the deep economic change at the macro-level and the consequences for the situation of households as economic actors at the micro-level.

One basic micro-economic indicator for the extent of economic coping of post-Communist households is the analysis of the general economic state of the individual household before 1989 in comparison with the effects of an adaptation of household strategies after 1989. We analysed this phenomenon by asking all respondents if the overall economic situation of their own household got better or worse during the period since 1989 (see Table 5.1). The overall picture shows that approximately 60 per cent of all post-Communist households in Central and Eastern Europe are worse off today than before 1989, that is, they are still losers in the process

Table 5.1 Actual economic performance of household better or the same as 1989

Q. How do you compare your overall household economic situation with nine years ago? Better today; the same; or worse today.

Country	NDB 1 1991	NDB 2 1992	NDB 3 1994	NDB 4 1996	NDB 5 1998	Change
Central Europe	34	37	39	47	45	11
Czech Republic	47	49	50	61	54	7
Slovenia	20	38	47	55	50	30
Poland	39	32	38	50	49	10
Slovakia	32	38	37	41	46	14
Hungary	32	27	25	28	28	−4
Southern Europe	44	47	38	35	37	−7
Romania	53	47	44	34	41	−8
Bulgaria	34	46	41	41	40	6
Croatia	*	*	30	30	30	0
FR of Yugoslavia	*	*	*	*	14	*
Northern Europe	*	*	35	41	*	6
Estonia	*	*	46	57	*	11
Lithuania	*	*	30	37	*	7
Latvia	*	*	30	30	*	0
Eastern Europe	*	32	20	27	25	−7
Russia	43	48	31	42	44	1
Belarus	*	29	18	18	21	−8
Ukraine	*	20	12	22	10	−10

Note
*Not done in this country at this time.

of economic transformation from a planned economy towards a market economy. Nevertheless, the general impression concerning that micro-economic indicator is that the share of households, which are either in the same economic condition compared to 1989 or better off than before the dramatic changes at the end of the 1980s, increased between 1991 and 1998, albeit very slowly.

In 1991, only 37 per cent of all households in Central and Eastern Europe had the same or a better situation compared to their standard of living before 1989. Between 1992 and 1996 that figure oscillated around 40 per cent of all post-Communist households, whereas we find 42 per cent of households either better off or in the same condition as before the regime changes, in spring 1998.

The winner of a comparison between the Communist era and the post-Communist period are the Czech households: already 47 per cent of all Czech households were in the same or a better position regarding their standard of living in 1991 in comparison with 1989, a percentage which increased to 50 per cent in 1994 and an absolute majority of 61 per cent of all Czech households in 1996. The share of Czech households, which have the same level or a better level of material resources – compared to

1989 – in their own household, went down from 61 per cent in 1996 to 54 per cent in 1998, which indicates – after a long period of material improvement of Czech households between 1991 and 1996 – a perceived decline in the material resources of families and households in the Czech Republic between 1996 and 1998.

The second rank concerning the improvement of household living standards in comparison with the Communist economy is occupied by Slovenia: in 1991, only 20 per cent of the Slovenian households indicated that their economic position was better or the same compared to the past. However, the percentage of stable or improving households went down from 55 per cent to 50 per cent in spring 1998. Nevertheless, we can see that the Slovenian households show the highest speed of micro-economic improvements. A dynamic upward tendency is also visible in the Polish economy: at the beginning of the process of economic transformation, 39 per cent of all Polish households feel that their own household is either better off or in the same position in 1991 in comparison with the 1980s. This went up to 50 per cent in 1996 and remained stable at this level with 49 per cent in 1998. Generally, we can argue that one-half of the Polish households are better off or the same compared with their position under Communism, but the other half is in a worse material position than before 1989, having lost out in the economic changes so far. In Slovakia, the economic situation of the Slovak households has improved quite considerably since the end of Communism: in 1991, at an early stage of economic transition, only 32 per cent of all Slovakian households were subjectively better off or in the same position compared to 1989. This share of improving or stable Slovak households increased to 38 per cent in 1992 and to 41 per cent in 1996. The most recent figure from spring 1998 shows a further increase of improving and stable households within the Slovak economy – up to 46 per cent. Hence we have now a group of four, the Czech, Slovenian, Polish and Slovak economies, where between 46 and 54 per cent of all households can be described either as feeling better off after economic transformation or as having a stable position in a longitudinal perspective.

In Romania, the trend is somewhat different: at the beginning of the transformation process in 1991, 53 per cent of the Romanian households had the subjective evaluation that they were either better off or had the same standard of living compared to the last years of the Romanian Communist regime. This comparatively high share of stable or improving households decreased during transition to 44 per cent in 1994 and finally to 34 per cent in 1996. This general downward trend was stopped in 1996: the percentage of winning or stable Romanian households went up from 34 per cent in 1996 to 41 per cent in 1998. In Bulgaria, the trend is again different: in 1991, only 34 per cent of the Bulgarian households had the impression that their micro-economic position was better or the same in comparison to the centrally planned Bulgarian economy. There was a sharp increase from one-third of improving and stable Bulgarian house-holds in 1991 to 46 per cent in 1992. This high level of economic satisfac-tion, if compared with the situation of the household before the changes, has never been reached again in Bulgaria. Between 1994 and 1998, we see the clear picture of stagnation regarding the share of winning or stable households in Bulgaria at about 40 per cent. This fact implies that we have between 1994 and 1998 a constant group of 60 per cent of all Bulgarian households, which are in a worse material position in comparison with the Bulgarian planned economy before 1989. In Croatia, the overall situation of households is very stable during the process of transition: a constant number of 30 per cent of all Croatian households has either a stable stan-dard of living compared to the Yugoslavian economy or has currently a higher level of material household resources. The great majority of 70 per cent of all Croatian households take the view that their economic position is worse now than before 1989. The case of Hungary is special, because the reference of comparison is the Hungarian economy of the 1980s, which is regarded by large parts of the Hungarian population as the 'golden era' of Hungarian history in the twentieth century. In 1991, only 32 per cent of the Hungarian households were either benefiting from the changes or could be labelled as stable households. This share of improv-ing or stable Hungarian households went down further to 27 per cent in 1992 and 25 per cent in 1994. During the last four years between 1994 and 1998, the percentage of improving or stable Hungarian households grew slowly to 28 per cent and remained at that rather modest level of the Hun-garian standard of living, as compared with the Hungarian living con-ditions during the 1980s. The situation of households in Serbia and Montenegro in spring 1998 is generally much worse than before 1989: only 14 per cent of the Serbian and Montenegrinian households have the subjective perception that their own household is either the same as before the changes or even better. This fact implies that 86 per cent of all households in Serbia and Montenegro are worse off in 1998 in compari-son with the life in former Yugoslavia.

The participation of post-Communist households in the formal and the informal economies

Another important element of a successful transformation towards a market economy consists in the share of the newly established formal or regular economy compared to all economic activities. The higher the penetration of the new economic system with the formal economy, which is regular jobs, payment of taxes and social insurance, etc., the more advanced is the process of transition towards a fully-fledged market economy. If the informal sector is very large, which means that people do not pay taxes, do not contribute to social and health insurance schemes and have irregular jobs, then the structure of the emerging market economy is lagging behind. The first aim of the following indicator is to get an impression of how many households are already integrated in the formal and regular economy and what is the size of the informal economy in a given post-Communist country.

We measure the extent of penetration of the economic structure by the formal and regular economy by asking the households, if they are able to get enough money by a regular economic activity within the formal economy, or if the portfolio of the specific household is relying entirely or additionally upon economic activities in the informal economy in order to have a satisfying standard of living. At the beginning of the New Democracies Barometer in 1991, an average of 37 per cent of all Central and Eastern European households was able to enjoy a satisfactory standard of living on the basis of a regular income that is either a regular salary or a pension or other public transfers as part of social and welfare policies (see Table 5.2). This share of households, which could live basically with one or more regular incomes, grew over time to 39 per cent in 1992 and to 42 per cent in 1994. Since 1994 that percentage has remained roughly at the same level of about 40 per cent of all households, which could get by exclusively with a regular salary or other forms of regular income. The

Table 5.2 Getting by with regular job/income

Q. Do you get enough money from your regular job to buy what you really need?

Country	NDB 1 1991	NDB 2 1992	NDB 3 1994	NDB 4 1996	NDB 5 1998	Change 1991–8
Central Europe	38	42	48	42	55	17
Slovenia	41	58	58	45	63	22
Czech Republic	46	53	58	55	58	12
Slovakia	39	38	46	32	53	14
Poland	38	34	43	41	52	14
Hungary	25	26	34	37	49	24
Southern Europe	36	34	32	34	20	−16
FR of Yugoslavia	*	*	*	*	38	*
Croatia	*	28	27	18	26	−2
Bulgaria	28	29	24	36	17	−11
Romania	44	44	45	48	16	−28
Northern Europe	*	*	22	25	*	3
Lithuania	*	*	25	31	*	6
Estonia	*	*	24	29	*	5
Latvia	*	*	18	16	*	−2
Eastern Europe	*	19	17	10	14	−5
Belarus	*	22	20	*	22	0
Russia	31	13	15	7	11	−20
Ukraine	*	23	17	12	8	−15

Note
* Not done in this country at this time.

Fifth New Democracies Barometer in spring 1998 showed that 42 per cent of all Central and Eastern European households could survive as part of the official economy, on the one hand, and the official welfare state, on the other. That result has the important implication that almost 60 per cent of all Central and Eastern European households are unable to get by financially on the basis of regular salaries or regular pensions. These households are forced to develop a whole portfolio of micro-economic activities beyond and outside of the official economy in order to survive the process of economic transformation.

The best micro-economic situation of households could be found between 1991 and 1996 in the Czech Republic. At the beginning of the transformation process in 1991, 46 per cent of all Czech households were able to get by just by using the regular income or regular pension. In 1992, the majority of all Czech households (53 per cent) got by with regular incomes. This share went up to 58 per cent in 1994 and has remained at this level ever since. The second best micro-economic performance of households is found in Slovenia: already in 1992, an absolute majority of 58 per cent of Slovenian households could survive exclusively on the basis of regular incomes and/or regular transfer payments by the welfare state. In spring 1998, Slovenia overtook the Czech Republic in terms of micro-economic performance of households with regard to the official economy: 63 per cent of Slovenian households indicated that they get enough money from regular jobs or, for example, regular pensions in order to buy all the things they need for their livelihood. Between 1991 and 1998, the share of Slovenian households able to survive with their participation within the official economy or the official welfare state, increased from 41 per cent to 63 per cent, which appears to be quite remarkable.

The third place in the ranking of the micro-economic performance of post-Communist households is occupied by Slovakia: at the beginning of economic transformation in Slovakia in 1991, only 39 per cent of all Slovakian households were able to survive economically through their participation in the Slovakian official economy or the Slovakian welfare state. This share went up over the years to 53 per cent of all Slovak households which got by on regular incomes or regular pensions. In terms of the micro-economic performance of households, we can speak of a convergence between Czech and Slovak households, the latter showing a higher growth than the former. Almost an identical pattern to the Slovak situation can be observed in Poland: in 1991, only 38 per cent of all Polish households got by within the official economy, whereas in 1998 already the absolute majority of 52 per cent of all Polish households were able to survive economically with regular incomes and/or regular welfare payments.

The Hungarian households hold the fifth rank of post-Communist households: in 1991, only 25 per cent of all Hungarian households were able to survive within the official Hungarian economy and the official Hungarian welfare state. Up to 1998, that share rose quite dramatically to 49 per cent of all Hungarian households, which now have enough money from a regular job or a regular pension in order to maintain a certain standard of living. The change over time is highest in Hungary with an increase of 24 per cent of households which get by within the official economy, followed by Slovenia, where the increase is 22 per cent. In five countries of Central Europe the number of households which are able to get by economically either as part of the official economy or as part of the official welfare state, is growing constantly during the process of economic transformation between 1991 and 1998. The most positive and encouraging micro-economic developments are visible in Slovenia, the Czech Republic, Slovakia, Poland and Hungary. Beyond the Central European buffer zone of the above-mentioned countries the micro-economic trend is less encouraging: in Croatia, Bulgaria and Romania the number of households which are able to survive as actors in the official economy or the official welfare state shrank between 1991 and 1998. In the Federal Republic of Yugoslavia, 38 per cent of all households get by on the basis of regular incomes; we have no previous comparisons for Yugoslavia, because our first survey was conducted in 1998. In Croatia, 28 per cent of all Croatian households could survive with official jobs and official pensions in 1992, but only 26 per cent of all Croatian households got by in this way in 1998. In spring 1998, 74 per cent of all Croatian households had to develop an individual portfolio of household activities in order to survive financially. In the Eastern European countries of Bulgaria and Romania the share of households which are coping financially within the official economy decreased between 1991 and 1998: in Bulgaria, 28 per cent of all households had enough money from regular incomes in 1991. The figure declined to 17 per cent of all Bulgarian households in 1998. That implies that 83 per cent of the Bulgarian households have to have a household strategy well beyond the official economy if they want to survive financially. In Romania, we notice a steep decline from 44 per cent of all Romanian households, which get by with regular incomes, in 1991, down to 16 per cent of Romanian households in 1998. The overall picture is that we can observe a divergence of micro-economic developments in Central and Eastern Europe: in Central Europe, the impact and the influence of the official economy and the welfare system are increasing, the micro-economic behaviour of Central European households (Czech Republic, Hungary, Poland, Slovakia, Slovenia) is 'normalising', whereas in Southern Europe (Croatia, Federal Republic of Yugoslavia) and in Eastern Europe (Bulgaria, Romania) the impact of the official economy upon the micro-economic behaviour of households is shrinking and supplemented more and more by a whole portfolio of household strategies beyond the official economy and outside the public welfare system.

The share of consolidated households

The second stage of transformation after the period of creation of the market economy and democracy consists in the process of consolidation of the new political, economic and social structures. This applies at the micro-economic level also to individual households. We tried to operationalise the economic consolidation of post-Communist households by the two following questions. The first related indicator of the micro-economic consolidation of post-Communist households is the percentage of families who get by financially and are even able to save some money during the year. At the beginning of the process of economic transformation in 1991, an average of 63 per cent of all Central and Eastern European households were able to maintain their standard of living and some of those households even managed to save money. The share of households with those characteristics is growing very slowly: in 1998, we find that 66 per cent of all households got by economically or were able to make savings (see Table 5.3).

We find the highest number of households which either get by financially or made some savings in Hungary during the first years of

Table 5.3 The share of consolidated households getting by and making savings with household portfolio

Q. In the past year has your family made savings, or just got by or spent some savings or borrowed money or spent savings and borrowed money?

Country	NDB 1 1991	NDB 2 1992	NDB 3 1994	NDB 4 1996	NDB 5 1998	Change 1991–8
Central Europe	69	67	71	68	72	3
Hungary	68	64	67	66	77	9
Czech Republic	71	72	72	75	76	5
Poland	74	62	69	60	74	0
Slovenia	69	70	78	69	68	0
Slovakia	62	65	67	68	66	4
Southern Europe	49	55	56	51	56	7
FR of Yugoslavia	*	*	*	*	67	*
Croatia	*	58	62	57	65	7
Bulgaria	42	45	46	45	53	11
Romania	56	61	61	*	51	−5
Northern Europe	*	*	71	71	*	0
Estonia	*	*	73	73	*	0
Latvia	*	*	74	70	*	−4
Lithuania	*	*	67	70	*	3
Eastern Europe	*	64	65	53	53	−9
Russia	62	75	77	60	63	1
Belarus	*	61	62	45	61	0
Ukraine	*	55	55	*	42	−13

Notes
* Not done in this country at this time.
Percentage making savings + getting by.

transformation, but Hungary was always well behind the Czech Republic, Poland and Slovenia. Nevertheless, the share of consolidated households in Hungary went up steeply from 66 per cent in 1996 to 77 per cent of all Hungarian households in 1998. Between 1991 and 1998, the Czech households almost always had the best micro-economic performance using that subjective indicator: already in 1991, 71 per cent of all Czech households indicated that they were already financially consolidated. That share rose very slowly in the course of the process of Czech economic reforms to 76 per cent in 1998, which gives the Czech households the second rank behind the Hungarian households. The third rank of post-Communist households is filled by Poland, where 74 per cent of all Polish households regard themselves as consolidated in spring 1998. That share of consolidated Polish households went up from 60 per cent in 1996 to 74 per cent in 1998, which indicates a clear-cut improvement of the economic conditions of Polish households during the past three years.

The position of Slovenian households is quite stable during the period of micro-economic transition: in 1991, 69 per cent of all Slovenian families were consolidated in 1998, 68 per cent of the Slovenian households displayed the same economic behaviour. Hence, we can speak of a constant percentage of 70 per cent of all Slovenian households, which are already consolidated. In the Federal Republic of Yugoslavia, 67 per cent of the households say that they can economically survive at a certain level.

We see high stability in the economic behaviour of Slovak households: the number of consolidated Slovak households rose slowly from 62 per cent in 1991 to 66 per cent in 1998. The Croatian households show improving economic conditions during the past three years: the percentage of consolidated Croatian households grew from 57 per cent in 1996 to 65 per cent in 1998. An interesting longitudinal pattern was discovered in Bulgaria: between 1991 and 1996, the share of consolidated households always moved between 42 per cent and 46 per cent of all Bulgarian households. In the course of the past three years we notice a visible increase of households with some financial stability from 45 per cent in 1996 up to 53 per cent in 1998, which gives some hope for the micro-economic future in Bulgaria at the level of households amidst a rather bleak overall picture of the Bulgarian national economy. The situation in Romania was consistently better in the first years of economic transformation, but we notice a decline between 1994 and 1998 from 61 per cent of consolidated Romanian households in 1994 to 51 per cent of Romanian households with some financial stability.

On average, one-third of all post-Communist households in Central and Eastern Europe are satisfied in a general way with the actual situation of their own family (see Table 5.4). The share of households with basic satisfaction about the current economic position of the family during the whole period between 1991 and 1998 is moving between 35 and 37 per cent of all households. That fact implies on the other hand that two-thirds

Table 5.4 Satisfaction with economic performance of household

Q. All in all how do you rate the economic situation of your family today?

Country	NDB 1 1991	NDB 2 1992	NDB 3 1994	NDB 4 1996	NDB 5 1998	Change 1991–8
Central Europe	34	39	37	38	43	9
Czech Republic	58	59	54	57	53	−5
Slovenia	28	45	48	42	53	25
Poland	17	23	25	35	44	27
Slovakia	46	47	39	35	40	−6
Hungary	23	20	19	21	25	2
Southern Europe	37	35	32	34	23	−14
Romania	37	33	33	42	33	−4
Croatia	*	33	30	33	25	−8
FR of Yugoslavia	*	*	*	*	22	*
Bulgaria	37	38	34	28	10	−27
Northern Europe	*	*	27	35	*	8
Estonia	*	*	37	41	*	4
Lithuania	*	*	25	40	*	15
Latvia	*	*	20	23	*	3
Eastern Europe	*	31	31	18	28	−3
Belarus	*	36	39	23	42	6
Russia	26	28	30	22	27	1
Ukraine	*	30	24	9	15	−15

Notes
* Not done in this country at this time.
Percentage very satisfactory + fairly satisfactory.

of all post-Communist households have been dissatisfied at different levels with the general economic and financial situation of their own household during the past ten years since the beginning of the process of economic transformation.

Up until recently, the Czech households showed by far the highest level of subjective satisfaction about the financial situation of the family: already at the beginning of economic transformation in the Czech society in 1991, 58 per cent of all Czech households indicated that they were either very satisfied or fairly satisfied with the economic performance of their own family. Between 1996 and 1998, the percentage of economically satisfied Czech households decreased from 57 to 53 per cent, showing a growing dissatisfaction in Czech households during the past three years.

The general satisfaction of the Slovenian households with the current economic situation of the household was quite low at the beginning of transition: only 28 per cent of all Slovenian households were satisfied with their economic situation in 1991. Over the years, the Slovenian households became more and more satisfied, in 1994 already 48 per cent of all Sloven-ian households expressed some satisfaction with the economic situation of the family in that year. In 1998, the group of very or fairly satisfied Slovenian households reached a record high with 53 per cent of Slovenian households, which brings this micro-economic indicator for Slovenia on a par with the Czech Republic, both countries leading in that respect.

The case of Poland is very interesting: the percentage of households with some degree of economic satisfaction rose between 1991 and 1998 in a linear and constant manner. At the beginning of economic transformation – 1991– only 17 per cent of all Polish households were satisfied with their economic situation. That share increased to 23 per cent in 1992, 25 per cent in 1994 and 35 per cent in 1996. In spring 1998 Polish households showed the highest level of economic satisfaction since 1990: 44 per cent of all Polish households were very or fairly satisfied with their own standard of living. In Slovakia, the pattern is quite different: in the earlier years of economic transition, there was quite a high number of Slovak households with good levels of economic satisfaction: in 1992, 47 per cent of the Slovak households were quite satisfied with the economic performance of the household. The share of satisfied Slovak households went down in the mid-1990s, but between 1996 and 1998 that percentage again showed an upward tendency: whereas in 1996, only 35 per cent of all Slovak households were satisfied with their standard of living, that percentage went up to 40 per cent of all Slovak households at the latest New Democracies Barometer in spring 1998.

The subjective standard of living in Romania and Croatia has been falling in recent years. Between 1991 and 1996, the percentage of satisfied Romanian households increased steadily from 37 per cent (1991) to 42 per cent (1996), but since 1996 that share has gone down from 42 per cent to 33 per cent, roughly one-third of all Romanian households, which are economically satisfied. The longitudinal pattern in Croatia was different again: between 1992 and 1996, an average of one-third of all Croatian households was very or fairly satisfied, but this percentage fell to 25 per cent in 1998. In Hungary, one-fifth of all Hungarian households had a satisfactory standard of living with values between 19 per cent and 23 per cent of the Hungarian households. The share of satisfied Hungarian households went up from 21 per cent in 1996 to 25 per cent in 1998, which is another sign of the economic upswing of the Hungarian economy at the micro-economic level. In the Federal Republic of Yugoslavia, only 22 per cent of all households in Serbia and Montenegro are fairly or very satisfied with their own standard of living, the remaining 78 per cent of the Serbian households are dissatisfied with the economic performance of their own household. Bulgaria is the only country out of all nine Central and Eastern European nations where we observe a consistent downwards trend during the process of economic transition. At the beginning of economic transition in 1991, 37 per cent of all Bulgarian households were fairly satisfied or very satisfied with their own standard of living. That share went down to 28 per cent in 1996 and reached an all-time low of 10 per cent of all Bulgarian households in 1998. In other words, 90 per cent of all Bulgarian households are dissatisfied with their financial and economic situation after nine years of economic transition, which should be labelled more as stagnation than as transformation.

Micro-economic well-being of households and democracy

The micro-economic situation of post-Communist households is more important for the process of democratisation than the dimension of social structure, which was analysed in Chapter 4. We have put together the main four elements of micro-economic well-being at the level of individual households in a multivariate model and calculated the influence of these four independent variables upon the dependent variable support for democracy (see Table 5.5). The micro-economic well-being of households explains altogether 13 per cent of the variance of the regression model, which is considerably more than the 4 per cent variance explained by social structure (see Chapter 4).

The most important micro-economic influence is visible predominantly in those post-Communist households, which have currently a better financial situation than before 1989. These micro-economic winners of economic transformations since 1989 display at the same time a considerable propensity to be democrats too. The association between being a winning household and democracy went up from +0.13 (= beta) in 1994 to +0.23 (= beta) in 1998. The experience of micro-economic and individual financial success, or at least economic stability, seems to be an important precondition for a general democratic orientation. The second most important micro-economic influence upon democracy consists in the overall satisfaction of Central and Eastern European citizens with the current economic condition of their own household. This link between being satisfied with the financial status quo of your household, on the one hand, and generalised support for democracy on the other, grew from +0.03 in 1994 to +0.16 in 1998. Obviously, overall satisfaction with the economic conditions of one's individual household is beneficial in supporting the form of regime at the same time, and where this is happening, this means the new democracy in post-Communist Europe. The third most important micro-economic factor for democratic support is the fact that a given household is getting by financially without having to spend

Table 5.5 Economic performance of households and democracy

	1994	1996	1998	Change
Current HH situation better than 1989	+0.13	+0.14	+0.23	+0.10
Current HH situation satisfactory	+0.03	+0.25	+0.16	+0.13
Well getting by	+0.08	+0.03	+0.07	−0.01
Enough from regular job	+0.06	+0.06	+0.03	−0.03
R^2	0.05	0.13	0.13	+0.08
Significance	0.00	0.00	0.00	0.00

their savings or borrow money from others outside the household. The association between financial coping of the household and democracy is constant during transition with a regression coefficient of approximately +0.07. Finally, the fact that in a given household the money coming from the official economy through either a regular job or an official pension, is decreasing in importance throughout the years of transformation is important. The association between sufficient money supply from the formal economy and support for democracy went down from +0.06 in 1994 to +0.03 in 1998, is *de facto* slowly disappearing as a factor influencing the process of democratisation. All four factors are nevertheless significant in the regression model discussed in this chapter and the degree of explained variance is going up from 5 per cent in 1994 to 13 per cent in 1998. One interesting and maybe surprising result of what this chapter has shown consists in the fact that the micro-economic performance of post-Communist households appears to be more influential for democratisation than the position in society either as man or woman or as young or old citizen. Another interesting outcome of the comparative analysis in this chapter is that an emerging democratic orientation is linked more with a general perception of the economic situation of their own household compared with the era before 1989, on the one hand, and with the general satisfaction with the actual economic situation, on the other. Democratic orientations appear to be associated with general and overall perceptions and levels of economic satisfaction as well as overall comparisons with the household situation in the Communist past and less with concrete financial cost–benefit calculations at the end of the year in terms of money spent and money saved, and less with the concrete financial balance sheets of a given household.

6 The birth of the market economy and democracy

Introduction

The specific characteristics of the post-Communist transition consist in the fact that we are witnessing not only a political transformation from a totalitarian regime to a pluralistic democracy, but at the same time an economic transformation from a planned command economy to a free market economy in Central and Eastern Europe. One of the deepest and most dramatic as well as most visible structural changes after 1989 consisted in the transformation from a centrally planned economy to a decentralised market economy in a very short period, the creation of entirely new economic actors and the building of new economic institutions and a legal framework to ensure the freedom of economic activity. Whereas there were historical examples of successful processes of democratisation, for example, in Greece, Spain and Portugal, to name a few members of the European Union, who have successfully managed the difficult transition from authoritarian rule towards democracy, Europe had no experience in transforming a planned economy into a market economy. Hence, the economic transformation after 1989 in Central and Eastern Europe was possibly even more difficult and cumbersome than the political transformation from a totalitarian regime to a pluralistic democracy.

The theoretical concept of the study of economic, social and political transformations in Central and Eastern Europe is based upon the theory of 'quality of life', which analyses the quality of life of citizens, the welfare of the individual members of society, e.g. their standard of living, their satisfaction with economic, social and political phenomena by using economic, social and political indicators. Those indicators can be objective indicators of the individual quality of life or subjective indicators of the personal perception of the quality of life. In this study we use exclusively subjective indicators derived from comparative academic survey research. In the scientific literature this concept is also known as 'social reporting', which goes well beyond social processes and includes economic and political processes in the scope of empirical and comparative analysis. This comparison has a longitudinal dimension, over time, and a territorial dimension by comparing nations and societies.

Farewell to the planned economy of Communism

One of the specific features of the transformation from Communism to post-Communism between 1989 and 1998, analysed in this book, is that we are witnessing not only a transition from non-democratic to democratic regimes, but also from planned economies to market economies. This complexity of transformation after 1989 of deep structural changes within politics and within the whole economy made it much more difficult for citizens in Poland, Hungary or Russia and in all the post-Communist countries to cope with transition than, for example, for Spanish or Greek citizens at the beginning of the third wave of democratisation. An important step in the success of market economy consisted in the rejection of the old economy under Communism, the centrally planned command economy.

Concerning the old economic system, we can quantify the extent of rejection of the former centralised and bureaucratic planned economy, which had operated in the countries analysed for up to seventy years, before it collapsed very quickly in 1989 (see Table 6.1). Table 6.1 represents a quantitative indicator of subjective attitudes in the form of an interval scale of rejection of the former planned economy. The indicator

Table 6.1 Rejection of the planned economy under Communism

Q. Here is a scale for ranking how the economy works: the top, +100, is the best; the bottom, −100, the worst. Where on this scale would you put the Socialist economy before the revolution of 1989?

Country	1991	1992	1994	1996	1998	Change 1991–8
Central Europe	35	28	32	31	33	−2
Poland	38	26	38	50	43	5
Czech Republic	49	44	49	42	40	−9
Slovakia	29	24	19	19	30	1
Slovenia	39	32	37	26	30	−9
Hungary	19	15	16	16	23	4
Southern Europe	38	35	33	32	40	2
Romania	38	30	32	35	55	17
Croatia	*	48	42	42	33	−15
Bulgaria	38	26	26	20	33	−5
FR of Yugoslavia	*	*	*	*	20	*
Northern Europe	*	*	17	20	*	3
Estonia	*	*	18	31	*	*
Lithuania	*	*	12	16	*	*
Latvia	*	*	20	13	*	*
Eastern Europe	*	15	17	7	13	−2
Russia	*	*	26	*	*	*
Belarus	*	14	17	7	16	2
Ukraine	*	16	17	6	9	−7

Notes
*Not done in this country at this time.
Percentage of people who give ratings between −100 and −10.

of rejection of the planned economy before 1989 gives the command economy a rating between −100 and −10, where −10 is somewhat negative and −100 is extremely negative.

The rejection of the planned economy is highest in Southern Europe in 1998 with an average of 40 per cent of the citizens in Romania, Bulgaria or Croatia against the old economy before 1989. Also quite high is the negative evaluation of the command economy in Central Europe, where 33 per cent of post-Communist citizens express their dislike in 1998 for the planned economy. In the Baltic countries, only 20 per cent are explicitly against the old economy in 1998. Only 13 per cent of post-Soviet citizens in Eastern Europe are definitely against the Soviet economy in 1998.

The only post-Communist country with an absolute majority of the population, which is against the command economy, happens to be Romania with 55 per cent of Romanians giving the command economy under Ceauşescu an overall negative rating. In all other fourteen post-Communist countries, the group of citizens who have definitely negative feelings about the planned economy are still a minority in 1998. In Romania we find strong hostility towards the old Romanian economy already in early stages of transformation. In 1991, 38 per cent of the Romanian population showed negative ratings for the partially bizarre economy, directed by Communist Party leader Ceauşescu. In Bulgaria and Croatia, we find one-third of the population clearly against the old economy. In Croatia, the rejection of the planned economy under Tito was much higher at the beginning of transition in 1992, when 48 per cent of the Croats showed their dislike of the late Yugoslav economy. The austerity and the hardships of the Croatian war economy under President Tudjman reduced the negative feelings towards the past and even fuelled some economic nostalgia for the macro-economy of the former Yugoslavia. In Bulgaria, the pattern was similar to Croatia: in 1991, 38 per cent of the Bulgarians gave the planned economy a negative evaluation, but the absence of economic reforms of the first Bulgarian government, run by the Bulgarian Socialist Party, alienated many Bulgarians from the new market economy and reduced their dislike for the economic past. In 1996, only 20 per cent of the Bulgarian electorate rejected the previous Bulgarian economy.

In Central Europe we find the highest levels of rejection of the past economy in Poland. In 1998, 43 per cent of all Poles showed their dislike of the Polish planned economy. A similar level of rejection of the old economy has been found in the Czech Republic, where 40 per cent of all Czechs gave the Czechoslovak command economy a negative rating in 1998. Between 1991 and 1994, even 49 per cent of the Czech electorate were against the planned economy of the past, but the economic and political crisis between 1996 and 1998 reduced the rejection of the past in the light of contemporary difficulties and disappointments for the Czech public.

The pattern in Slovakia is quite different from the pattern in the Czech Republic despite their joint past; both societies have different assessments of a common economic past in the former Czechoslovakia. In 1998, only 30 per cent of all Slovak citizens were clearly against the Czechoslovak command economy, which is considerably less than in Czech society. This share of one-third of the Slovak population, who reject the Czechoslovak economy, is constant between 1991 and 1998 with rather small fluctuations. In Slovenia, we find a similar level of rejection of the planned economy to that in Slovakia. In 1998, 30 per cent of all Slovenes show their dislike of the Yugoslav economy, where Slovenia was paying more than receiving from the national budget. Within Central Europe, the case of Hungary is deviant because of the specific context of economic transformation in this country. During the 1980s the Hungarian economy under János Kádár was rather successful in combining socialist and capitalist elements and was hence regarded by a considerable segment of Hungarian society as a 'golden era' in Hungarian history. This special Hungarian way of organising the economy was supported by many Hungarians and the arrival of the market economy after 1989 was hence rather disappointing for many Hungarians. This special Hungarian situation resulted in a very low rate of rejection of the old economy in Hungary. In 1991, only 19 per cent of the Hungarian electorate were against the former Hungarian economy. This share increased only slightly between 1991 and 1998 to 23 per cent.

Within the Baltic region, we find a considerable rejection of the former Soviet economy only in Estonia, where 31 per cent of the population gave the planned Soviet economy a negative rating in 1996. In Lithuania and Latvia, the Soviet economy was rejected by around 15 per cent of the electorates, which appears to be rather low. A similar pattern to that in Latvia and Lithuania occurs in Belarus and the Ukraine. In Belarus a constant share of 16 per cent of the population rejected the Soviet economy between 1992 and 1998, which is not too surprising because this planned economy survived in many parts under the regime of President Lukashenka. In the Ukraine the Soviet economy was rejected by 16 per cent in 1994 and only by 9 per cent in 1998. The apparent failure to introduce a functioning market economy in the Ukraine during the 1990s obviously caused some nostalgia for the stability of the former Soviet system, especially the social stability of regular incomes and pensions and the absence of unemployment.

Support for the market economy

How do ordinary citizens perceive the transformation of a planned economy to a market economy? The success of a transition of that scope depends upon the favourable reaction of the general public. Only when the population of a post-Communist country is prepared to accept the basic features of that macro-economic transformation, can we speak of a successful transition process. The feedback of the population in the form of positive signals is necessary to assess the speed and intensity of popular acceptance of the path towards an emerging market economy. Transformation research has the task of measuring the support for the old economic system of a planned economy, on the one hand, and the support for the emerging new market economy, on the other hand, and to compare those different levels of popular support for economic systems. In this context it is important to note that the changes in the economic system between 1989 and 1998 are not a transition from A to B, where the form and structure of B are already known. I prefer to speak of an open process of transformation, where the starting point is known, but not the end point. The term transition is therefore conceptually wrong, because it implies that we know where the economic changes are heading, which in fact nobody knows. We analyse the support of the population for the previous planned economy and for the current market economy in all fifteen Central and Eastern European countries by asking the following question:

Here is a scale for ranking how the economy works. The top, $+100$, is the best; at the bottom, -100, is the worst.
a. Where on this scale would you put the current economy?
b. Where on this scale would you put the economy in five years' time?

These questions represent a quantitative indicator of subjective attitudes in the form of an interval scale of retrospective satisfaction with the level of current satisfaction with the evolving market economy. The question measures popular support for a specific economic system.

Support for the current economy is not best measured by assessing the distance of the existing economic system in one country to an ideal-type of market economy which is very hard to identify anyway. The model of an open transformation, which is the conceptual basis of our longitudinal research programme in Central and Eastern Europe, means monitoring economic change by analysing the reactions of the general public, not the elites or experts, of a given economy. We do not analyse the views of the ordinary people about idealised or perfect market economy, but rather about the market economy which they experience every day, at work, as consumers or in performing other economic activities. The basic concept for analysing economic change in post-Communist societies relies upon the micro-economic behaviour, values and attitudes of the population in a given country, on the one hand, and the macro-economic experiences and expectations of a given general public on the other. The process of macro-economic and micro-economic transformation in Central and Eastern Europe could be labelled a success only when the majority of any population supports their specific market economy and a large group silently accepts it. Such a majority of open supporters and neutrals, who accept the outcome of the reform process, can ensure that economic reform has reached the light at the end of the tunnel of transformation.

Support for the new market economy in Central and Eastern Europe has been growing during the process of economic transformation since 1989 (see Table 6.2). In 1991, at the beginning of the New Democracies Barometer, 34 per cent of all Central and Eastern Europeans displayed a positive evaluation of the very new market economy in their own country. If one considers the fact that after two years of transformation already one-third of the population supported the market economy, this appears to be quite astonishing and shows the high hopes and expectations of many 'ordinary people', their deep desire for radical changes or for an economic revolution. The number of post-Communist citizens who had a favourable opinion about the emerging market economy went down

Table 6.2 Support for the current market economy (or current economic system)

Q. Here is a scale for ranking how the economy works. The top, +100, is the best; at the bottom, −100, is the worst. Where on this scale would you put the current market economy?

Country	NDB 1 1991	NDB 2 1992	NDB 3 1994	NDB 4 1996	NDB 5 1998	Change 1991–8
Central Europe	36	38	44	53	42	6
Poland	31	39	50	68	61	30
Slovenia	18	35	48	55	40	22
Hungary	37	29	27	27	40	3
Czech Republic	57	55	66	71	38	−19
Slovakia	41	34	31	43	31	−10
Southern Europe	28	26	29	34	28	0
Bulgaria	23	24	15	23	35	12
Romania	33	32	35	37	27	−6
Croatia	*	22	37	42	21	−1
FR of Yugoslavia	*	*	*	*	17	*
Northern Europe	*	*	33	37	*	4
Estonia	*	*	55	63	*	8
Lithuania	*	*	19	27	*	8
Latvia	*	*	26	21	*	−5
Eastern Europe	*	9	10	18	26	17
Belarus	*	15	11	16	38	23
Russia	*	9	14	22	31	22
Ukraine	*	4	6	15	10	6

Notes
*Not done in this country at this time.
Percentage of people with positive attitudes: +10 to +100.

slightly to 29 per cent in 1992. Between 1992 and 1996, support for the market economy increased from 29 per cent to 40 per cent. In spring 1998, we find an average of 37 per cent of people in Central and Eastern Europe who supported the market economy and were positive towards economic transformation. The small decrease between 1996 and 1998 is due to temporary, but not structural, economic dissatisfaction in the Czech Republic, Slovakia, Slovenia and Romania.

We find the highest level of support for the market economy in Poland: the satisfaction of the Polish population with the current state of the economy was very low in 1991, when only 31 per cent were positive about the Polish macro-economic situation. Since 1991, support for the Polish market economy has been growing steadily, up to 68 per cent of the Polish population supporting the current Polish economy in 1996. The form and course of economic reform in Poland during the first half of the 1990s caused a linear growth in support for the market economy in Poland. In Slovenia, the longitudinal pattern is very similar to Poland, albeit at a lower level: only 18 per cent of the Slovenian population supported the market economy in 1991, but that percentage went up steeply in 1992 to 35 per cent and in 1994 to 48 per cent. The peak of support for the market economy was finally reached in 1996, when the majority of 55 per cent of all Slovenians showed their support for the new market economy in Slovenia. The pattern of support for the market economy in Hungary is very peculiar if analysed over time: at the beginning of the reform process, 37 per cent of the Hungarian population supported the market economy, with which they were to some extent already familiar because of the economic reforms during the 1980s. Nevertheless, we find between 1992 and 1996 only 30 per cent of Hungarians evaluate the Hungarian reform economy in a positive way. We are witnessing a sharp upswing in support for the market economy in Hungary between 1996 and 1998, when the share of Hungarian supporters of the new economy went up from 27 per cent to 40 per cent. The subjective evaluation of the Czech economy was the highest throughout the period between 1991 and 1996: in 1991, the absolute majority of 57 per cent of the Czech population supported the new economic system: an amazing figure just two years after the end of Communism! The support for market economy went even higher to 66 per cent in 1994 and 71 per cent 1996, which was the highest value ever achieved for support for the market economy in the whole period of economic transformation in any country. Our studies give the impression that in 1996 the first period of transformation was over, that Central and Eastern Europe were now entering the second stage, which is closer to economic cycles as we know them from other OECD countries. The economic and political crisis in the Czech Republic in 1997 and 1998 resulted in a steep decline of support for the current Czech economy from 71 per cent in 1996 to 38 per cent in 1998. The market economy and its basic elements are now well embedded in Czech society and not in danger of being challenged as a value system. During the second stage of transition this indicator now measures the level of satisfaction of the Czech population with the performance of the Czech economy and with the outcome of the economic policies of the Czech government. In Bulgaria, support for the market economy produces a V-shaped curve: in 1991, 23 per cent of the Bulgarian population supported the slowly emerging market economy in Bulgaria; this low support practically collapsed in 1994, when only 15 per cent had any positive views on the Bulgarian economic system. Since 1994, the support for market economy has been slowly recovering with 23 per cent in 1996, but 35 per cent Bulgarian supporters in 1998. The political and economic changes in Bulgaria in 1997 and 1998 resulted in a strong increase of support for the market economy in Bulgaria. In Slovakia, support for the market economy oscillates between 30 and 40 per cent of the population. In 1998, only 31 per cent of the Slovak population evaluate the current state of market economy in Slovakia in a positive way. Romania had a slow but steady growth of support for the market economy from 33 per cent in 1991 to 37 per cent in 1996, but in 1998 support for the Romanian economy fell to 27 per cent, indicating decreasing satisfaction with the actual Romanian economic system. In Croatia, the number of supporters of the market economy grew from 22 per cent in 1992 in a linear fashion to 42 per cent in 1996. The effect of the war economy produced a reduction in popular support for the Croatian economy from 42 per cent in 1996 to 21 per cent in 1998. By far the lowest level of support for the market economy is found in the Federal Republic of Yugoslavia, where only 17 per cent have positive views of the Yugoslav economy.

Optimism about the market economy

After the successful birth of a market economy the next crucial step in the process of economic transformation is to consolidate the new economic system in a long-term perspective. The market economy has to be supported by a majority of citizens in order to survive in the long run and prevent a switch to other or – even worse – old economic systems, a return to some form of planned economy. A crucial indicator for the long-term support of the new market economy within the populace is widespread optimism about the successful future of the new economy in their own country in the foreseeable future, say, in the time span of the next five years (see Table 6.3). The assumption here is that if a majority of the population is confident about the positive development of the new market economy and optimistic about the chances for that macro-economic system surviving the next years of economic transformation, then there are quite good chances not only for mere survival, but also a sustainable development of the market economy in a given post-Communist country. The future market economy is supported by an absolute majority of post-

Table 6.3 Optimism about the future of the market economy

Q. Here is a scale for ranking how the economy works: the top, +100, is the best; the bottom, −100, the worst. Where on this scale would you put our economic system in five years?

Country	1991	1992	1994	1996	1998	Change 1991–8
Central Europe	58	60	73	75	62	+4
Poland	41	41	70	86	70	+29
Czech Republic	80	78	86	87	61	−19
Slovakia	65	65	73	72	56	−9
Slovenia	62	66	75	75	54	−8
Hungary	53	51	63	55	69	+16
Southern Europe	63	58	70	65	58	−5
Romania	63	60	66	64	54	−9
Croatia	*	63	71	58	51	−12
Bulgaria	64	50	72	72	69	+5
FR of Yugoslavia	*	*	*	*	45	*
Northern Europe	*	*	67	63	*	−4
Estonia	*	*	85	80	*	−5
Lithuania	*	*	53	58	*	+5
Latvia	*	*	62	50	*	−12
Eastern Europe	*	38	46	46	52	+14
Russia	*	42	44	40	45	+3
Belarus	*	33	48	57	64	+31
Ukraine	*	38	45	40	48	+10

Notes
* Not done in this country at this time.
Percentage of people who give ratings between +10 and +100.

Communist societies in Central Europe, in Southern Europe, but also in the Baltics. The deviant case is Eastern Europe, where the future expectations regarding the market economy are not as optimistic as in the other three regions within post-Communist Europe.

The average number of Central Europeans who are optimistic about the future development of the market economy increased from 58 per cent in 1991 to 62 per cent in 1998. The peak of Central European macroeconomic optimism was in 1996, when 75 per cent of all Central Europeans were confident about a bright mid-term future for the new economic system. In 1998, the 'normal' cycles of economic pessimism and optimism arrived in the post-Communist countries; there was no longer dispute about the market economy and its alternatives, the Central European economies joined in normal cycles of economic expectations like the other societies in the European Union. Regarding the extent of optimism about the future of the market economy, Poland is the first country among the fifteen post-Communist states analysed. In 1991, only 41 per cent of Polish citizens showed confidence in the emerging market economy, but in 1998 this share of Polish optimists increased to 70 per cent. One might postulate that the market economy is well embedded and accepted in Polish society after a decade of economic transition. Acceptance of the market economy and its principles was very high throughout the whole period of economic transformation in the Czech Republic with an average of 80 per cent of Czech citizens who were confident about the introduction and persistence of market economy in the Czech Republic. The economic and political crisis during the government of Prime Minister Klaus dampened the extremely optimistic economic mood in Czech society and reduced this share of mid-term optimists from 87 per cent in 1996 to 61 per cent in 1998 (Haerpfer and Wallace 1998). In Slovakia we find a constant share of 70 per cent of the population who are confident about the healthy development of the Slovak market economy during the 1990s. In the dusk of the government of Prime Minister Meciar, the share of Slovak optimists decreased from 72 per cent in 1996 to 56 per cent in spring 1998. In a similar way we see a constant majority of 70 per cent of Slovenes being optimistic about the future of market economy and its principles in the future between 1991 and 1996. As in Slovakia and the Czech economy, the share of optimists fell between 1996 and 1998, in the case of Slovenia from 75 per cent to 54 per cent. The Hungarian case is again special, because of the specific historical context for transition in Hungary. In 1991, only 53 per cent of the Hungarian population displayed some optimism about the new economic order, but during the 1990s acceptance of a full market economy in spite of a mixed economy as occurred in Hungary in the 1980s became more widespread. The optimism within Hungarian society regarding the mid-term future of the new market economy was already shared by 69 per cent of all Hungarians in 1998.

Whereas the economic optimism in Central Europe was supported by economic growth and improvements, the economic optimism in Southern Europe was supported mainly by hope and much less by real economic change. In Romania, for example, 63 per cent declared themselves to be optimistic about the future of market economy in 1991 despite a deep economic crisis after the collapse of the Ceaușescu regime. In the course of the 1990s, a constant group of 60 per cent of all Romanians kept their economic optimism without lasting economic improvements in this poverty-stricken country. In 1998 we still find 54 per cent of the Romanian electorate full of optimism about the macro-economic recovery of the Romanian economy. In Bulgaria, the gap between very poor economic conditions and the expression of economic optimism by around 70 per cent of all Bulgarians is even more striking. In the case of Romania and Bulgaria, one might argue in this respect that the status of an accession country of the European Union provides these peoples on the shores of the Black Sea with a ray of hope of macro-economic recovery, though in the distant future. Croatia was a society at war during the 1990s, which distorted the results to some extent: in 1994 71 per cent of Croatians declared themselves to be optimistic about the market economy in Croatia despite a deep economic crisis in the aftermath of the post-Yugoslav wars, high levels of unemployment and very low industrial output of the Croatian economy. This 'war bias' disappeared slowly from my New Democracy Barometer surveys and I finally found a share of 51 per cent of optimists regarding the future of market economy in Croatia in 1998.

Within the Baltic region, Estonia displays an outstanding level of macro-economic optimism in the mid-1990s. In 1996, the vast majority of 80 per cent of all Estonians express their optimism about the future thriving of the market economy in Estonia. This very high acceptance of the new economic system might be supported by the geographical closeness of Finland and other Scandinavian countries as well as with the high speed of economic integration around the Gulf of Finland. In Latvia and Lithuania, the expectations of the performance of the market economy within the next five years are much lower than in Estonia. Within the CIS region, we find very similar patterns of economic optimism, which are all well below the levels of optimism observed in Central or Southern Europe. The comparatively highest economic optimism was identified in Belarus. In 1992, only 33 per cent of the Byelorussians were optimistic about the new economic system, this share went up to 64 per cent in 1998. In the Russian Federation, the acceptance of the new economic structures is rather constant over time: approximately 40 per cent of the Russian population is optimistic about the future development of the Russian economy. In the Ukraine the economic climate improved from a very low level of 38 per cent of optimistic Ukrainians in 1992 to 48 per cent of the Ukrainian population in 1998, who had a positive outlook regarding the economy in the Ukraine.

Market economy and democracy

When these different elements of support for the emerging market economy in post-Communist countries are put together in one multivariate model, we discover first of all that the development of the market economy has a higher impact upon democratisation than social structure (Chapter 4) or the micro-economic performance of the post-Communist households (Chapter 5). The assessment of the macro-economic system in the Communist, the post-Communist present and the future by the general public in eleven Central and Eastern European countries explains 27 per cent of the variance of Democratisation (see Table 6.4). The most important predictor in the regression model with three crucial macro-economic indicators as independent variables and support for democracy as dependent variable happens to be the rejection of the old command economy. The regression coefficient of the influence of a negative assessment of the former economy for democratisation is –0.31.

The second most important dimension consists in optimism about the positive and successful development of the market economy in the future

Table 6.4 Market economy and democracy

	1994	1996	1998	Change
Rating Socialist economic system	−0.24	−0.29	−0.31	+0.07
Rating market economy	+0.10	0.20	+0.19	+0.09
Rating market economy in future	+0.25	0.22	+0.22	−0.03
R^2	0.18	0.27	0.27	+0.09
Significance	0.000	0.000	0.000	0.00

(beta = 0.22). Also quite important is a positive rating of the current market economy in post-Communist Europe. The impact of a positive evaluation of the current macro-economic structure upon support for democracy is +0.19. One might postulate on the basis of the outcomes of this chapter that a clear separation from the macro-economic past, strong support for the actual market economy and a lot of optimism for the future success of the market economy and its principles are the most decisive factors for the successful process of democratisation in Central and Eastern Europe after 1989. On the basis of this analysis I might conclude that the economy appears to matter more than politics regarding the impact upon the crucial process of democratisation in post-Communist Europe. This hypothesis is restricted to the micro-level of comparative analysis, the level of the post-Communist citizen in particular, and the general public in Central and Eastern Europe in general.

7   Security and democracy

Security issues in East and Central Europe have received a high profile recently with the entry of the three post-Communist countries Poland, Hungary and the Czech Republic into NATO and discussion about further widening this alliance. The collapse of Communism and the dissolution of the Warsaw Pact have brought new military alignments and potentialities. However, with the transformation of these countries into democratic societies, the views of the population also need to be taken into account. In this chapter we report the security-specific results of the New Democracies Barometer, a longitudinal, representative sample survey of ten post-communist countries in East and Central Europe: Hungary, Poland, the Czech and Slovak Republics, the Ukraine, Belarus, Bulgaria, Romania, Slovenia and Croatia. This chapter compares results of questions about attitudes to external and internal security in 1992 and 1998 in each of these countries. In particular, we consider subjective perceptions of threat from neighbouring countries, from great powers such as Russia, Germany and the USA, from national minorities and ethnic groups and from migrants and refugees. In this context I analyse their views on NATO membership. I compare these countries in general by constructing an index of perceptions of threat.

The end of the Cold War following the extraordinary political events in Eastern Europe in the late 1980s served to reshape the political and military map of Europe. In the words of George Bush, it augured a 'New World Order'. Previously the Iron Curtain had divided Europe into two halves, East and West, Communist and capitalist, NATO and Warsaw Pact. The break-up of the Warsaw Pact, the collapse of Communism and the disintegration of the Soviet Union into different states dissolved this neat divide which was set up after the Second World War.

For the countries of Central Europe, traditionally a military 'buffer zone' between East and West, it required some re-thinking of *external* security issues – who was now an enemy and who was a friend? This was as much a question for traditionally militarily neutral Austria as for the newly emerging democracies of Poland, the Czech and Slovak Republics, Hungary, Bulgaria and Romania. For those countries that had previously formed part of the Soviet Union but were now for the first time fully independent, these issues also arose. However, the opening of borders and the opening of societies also threw up new *internal* security issues as states began to fissure and re-align, populations began to move once more around the region and ethnic minorities found new voices with which to put forward their claims.

Since the initial transformation period things have moved rapidly. Several elections have confirmed the position of democratically elected governments in Poland, Hungary, the Czech and Slovak Republics and these countries also have special associate membership status of the EU and some of them are scheduled to become members during the next round of EU enlargement. Privatisation policies and successful economic transformation are making these countries increasingly 'normal' parts of Western Europe. However, war in the former Yugoslavia sent those countries in a different direction, even diverging from one another, as relatively prosperous Slovenia looks more like one of the Visegrad countries mentioned above and is expected to join the European Union in the not too distant future. The break-up of Czechoslovakia in 1992 showed that there were also peaceful means of bringing about the fission of post-Communist countries. Romania and Bulgaria have not gone the way of the former Yugoslavia, but also aspire to European Union recognition. Furthermore, they have been diverging from one another as Romania goes ahead with a rather radical privatisation and reform policy while Bulgaria is just staggering out of a major economic crisis. Finally, Belarus and the Ukraine have struggled to introduce political and economic reforms, so far not very successfully. In this process the Ukraine has become more westward-looking while Belarus appears to be more eastward-looking in terms of strategic alliances and political co-operation.

While the political and military elite planned new meetings and alliances, the introduction of democratically elected governments meant that more attention had to be paid to the attitudes and values of the population. What was their opinion? Who did they see as friends and enemies? The answers to these questions can be found by looking at survey data making comparisons between countries and across time. Out of these eleven countries, ten were members of the former military transnational organisation of the Warsaw Pact; only Romania was not part of that transnational military organisation of European Communism after the Second World War. Some of the new democracies were part of other states before 1989, but they all share the Warsaw Pact historical experience. The end of the Warsaw Pact left a military vacuum between Slovenia and the Ukraine, which is now a much debated topic in international politics.

Sources of insecurity

What are the threats to Central European post-Communist peoples? Historically this region has been a buffer zone between different empires: the

French, German, Austrian, Russian/Soviet and Turkish empires all came and went, fighting different battles and imposing different kinds of rule. Borders and boundaries were changed many times, countries were created, countries were destroyed or countries were simply moved to a different place. The population comprises a complex patchwork of different ethnic groups, speaking many different languages, many of which have lasted a long time despite the comings and goings of various rulers. With the nationalistic movements arising during the nineteenth century, many of the peoples of Central Europe were able to codify and further establish their literary and cultural heritage and claim their own nationhood with geographical borders (Gellner 1983). But given the history of the region, these borders were always disputed. Recognition of the existing borders therefore (however arbitrarily drawn) was one of the first key security issues of the post-1989 settlement. This has been an issue in every post-Communist Central European country where neighbours can make historically justified claims upon territory – in other words, all of them. Neighbouring countries therefore pose a potential threat to the security of post-Communist states, which are no longer protected by grand strategic alliances.

The two most bruising experiences of invasion by different empires in recent memory were those of Germany from the West and Russia or the Soviet Union from the East. Central Europeans have very vivid memories of the brutal invasion of Germany during the 1930s and the massive destruction of people and homes that took place as a result. Fear of threat from Germany is therefore still a very lively issue. Central Europeans have equally bitter memories of their subsequent 'liberation' by the Soviet troops from the East who did not leave for another forty-five years. Countries which had been allies of Germany were punished and although this regime was not as bloodthirsty in most countries as had been the previous occupation by Germans, the political and economic straitjacket imposed by Communist systems and the appropriation of property and political freedoms were bitterly resented, leading to a string of uprisings in these countries in the post-Second World War period. Very tangible evidence of the Soviet presence was provided by large numbers of troops and military manoeuvres to protect the Western frontier of the Soviet Empire. These troops were also used to suppress internal uprisings such as that in 1968 in the Czech Republic, in 1956 in Hungary and in 1953 in East Germany. The disintegration of the Soviet Union has curbed the threats originating from the East and helped to ensure the independence of the Central European countries, but the political uncertainty and instability in Russia mean that it is still potentially a threat for these small re-created nations. Although the Russians themselves may be unwilling to re-create the military ambitions of the former Soviet Union, demagogic politicians such as Vladimir Zhirinovsky have the power to stir up popular feelings.

Although Germany and Russia are the two most immediate great powers to threaten Central European countries, the other great power, which has been part of the global division of Communism and capitalism, is the USA. The USA also stationed troops across the border in Western Europe, undertook military manoeuvres and trained its missiles on Central and Eastern European cities. The collapse of the Soviet empire is often seen as a victory for the Americans. America exerts a considerable influence in Central Europe through business investment, the cultural dominance of consumer culture and Hollywood movies and through sending in various experts to help transform the political and economic systems of Central Europe. The USA, traditionally portrayed as the enemy of Communism, might still be perceived as a threat in Central European countries.

Despite the various forms of deportation or destruction of ethnic populations which have taken place over the past seventy years, each country contains ethnic populations and minorities from other countries as well as its own (Gellner 1994). For each country, the national minorities belonging to the neighbouring country can be used to de-stabilise rather fragile regimes, as was done when Germany invaded Czechoslovakia in 1938 to 'save' the ethnic Germans who were living there and happened in both Serbia and Croatia in the recent war in Yugoslavia. These national minorities can therefore be seen as a kind of 'fifth column' inside the country. There is also a particular problem with what Gellner (1996) has termed 'dominant minorities'; that is, the minority populations, which had previously been dominant ethnic groups but which the receding tide of empire had left behind. These dominant minorities often regard themselves as superior to the other people in the countries in which they live and are not very inclined to accept a lesser minority status. Examples of these are Russians in the Baltic States or the Ukraine and Hungarians in Romania or Serbs and Croats in Bosnia.

The post-Cold War period has seen the eruption of various ethnic conflicts in the region, and for the first time the persecution of minorities such as gypsies and Muslims (which was always widespread) has become more publicised. Furthermore, ethnic minorities are trying to find their own voice within the newly constructed states and political leaders often resist this. In some cases these ethnic minorities are well established and form highly articulate lobbies for use of their own language, their own education, their own representation in the political system, as is the case of the Hungarians in Romania. However, new ethnic groups have been discovered or re-discovered as part of the liberalisation process and perhaps as a consequence of global tendencies towards multi-culturalism. Examples in the Central European Region would be the German minority in Poland, believed not to exist only eight years ago, but who have now formed their own political party. Other examples are the Ruthenians in Carpatho-Ukraine whose cause has been espoused by a small number of local intellectuals and a non-local Canadian academic (Hann 1995).

There is a potent dynamic, which involves the co-variance of nationalising groups, minorities living in other countries and newly emergent countries (Rogers Brubaker 1996). For these reasons, minorities can be a threat to the internal security of the country.

In the past, movement in the countries of Central Europe was very restricted, even for their own citizens and even more restricted for outsiders. The Iron Curtain sealed off these countries from East–West movements. However, the dismantling of the Iron Curtain has resulted in new population flows and new forms of mobility. The traditional flow of movement has been from East to West and this continues with Central Europeans working, studying and visiting European Union countries either legally or illegally. Citizens from the countries bordering the European Union can cross the 'green line' without much problem now. Tourists and shoppers travel in large numbers across the borders from West to East. However, the opening of borders also liberalised movement around the Central European region as large numbers of Russians and Ukrainians or people from even further afield arrive to work, to shop or to trade in the more prosperous countries of post-Communist Central Europe. Increasing discrepancies in the economic fortunes of the different post-Communist countries encourages this flow of people (Wallace 1998; Wallace *et al.* 1996). The main recipients of these new flows of people from the East have been the Central European countries of Poland, Hungary, and the Czech and Slovak Republics. In addition to people coming to work or trade, these countries started to become transit countries for migrants from outside the region trying to get into Western Europe – from China, from Pakistan and from Africa, for example. Tens of thousands were turned back from the border to be sent back to the last country which they entered – mostly the post-Communist countries of Central Europe. These became transit countries not just for illegal migrants but also for criminal networks in arms, drugs, prostitution and stolen art dealing. The European Union, keen to keep its borders safe and stable, has been active in helping to deal with these problems, involving increasing co-operation and intervention in the countries of Central Europe. In economic terms and in terms of migration these countries form a new kind of 'buffer zone' between East and West.

For many businessmen from further East, it is more convenient to set up operations in the cheaper but also less institutionalised and more corruption-prone post-Communist countries than to go directly into Western Europe, and these Central European countries have therefore become communications points in this respect (Wallace *et al.* 1996). Many Western companies and Western investors have also started to move into Central Europe, bringing their own strata of professional employees with them. Western European and US shops, banks and businesses have become increasingly common.

For people in Central European countries the increase in migration has coincided with an increase in crime and these two things are linked in the minds of many people. Furthermore, a wave of asylum seekers and refugees (not always officially declaring themselves as such) hit the Visegrad countries after the war broke out in Yugoslavia and after European Union countries started closing their doors to these refugees in 1992.

The Central European post-Communist countries have therefore experienced an influx of migrations and temporary mobility, unknown for some fifty years. This can also be seen as a source of threat and insecurity even though the numbers are relatively small compared to many Western European countries. The more affluent countries of the 'buffer zone' – Poland, Hungary, the Czech and Slovak Republics – have been the main targets of this migration both because of their borders with the European Union and because of their relative affluence and political stability compared with other countries to the East and South (see Wallace and Stola 2001).

Who are friends and who are enemies?

The change described above has left the countries of post-Communist Central Europe with the need to re-think their alliances. Their relatively weak position in political, economic and military terms means that they are vulnerable to many influences. They are mostly relatively small countries with unstable borders, which enhances this vulnerability. The strengthening and deepening of ties within the European Union create a strong block on the Western side although the military union has not been pursued, despite some discussions. The European Union represents a strong *economic* pole of attraction into whose orbit the countries of Central Europe are drawn, whether they like it or not (Wallace *et al.* 1997). Many of them aspire to join the European Union, although negotiations are underway to admit only ten candidates from post-Communist Europe: Bulgaria, the Czech Republic, Estonia, Hungary, Latvia, Lithuania, Poland, Romania, Slovakia and Slovenia.

The continuing military strength of Russia to the East is illustrated by its intervention in Chechnya, Moldova and the Caucasus as well as its sabre-rattling over the Black Sea fleet. To the west, NATO continues to be a strong military global force. The countries of Central Europe are caught in the middle with little military clout. Not surprisingly, many post-Communist Central European countries also aspire to join NATO, although only three – Poland, the Czech Republic and Hungary – are already full members of NATO.

Other strategic alliances have been proposed or constructed but do not seem to carry the same political, economic or military weight: CEFTA (Central European Free Trade Area), CEI (Central European Initiative), CSCE (Council for Security and Co-operation in Europe), the Baltic Council and the Council of Europe are all examples (Cowen-Karp 1993).

For this reason it is important to look at who the people of Central Europe regard as their friends and enemies in the new re-ordering of Europe. This forms the next part of the chapter.

Perceptions of threat

One crucial question of the future stability or instability of the historically shattered European region is the form and the speed of integration into different forms of military co-operation. The question of military integration is closely linked to the different perceptions of threat in eleven post-Communist countries, which are the territorial focus of the analysis. The New Democracies Barometer asked in 1992 (= NDB 3), in 1996 (= NDB 4) and in 1998 (= NDB 5), which countries or other actors pose a threat to the country of the respondent. The results for the average of all eleven countries show a rather clear picture (see Table 7.1).

The greatest threat from a general public perspective for the post-Communist countries between Zagreb and Kiev appears to be Russia. The percentage of Eastern Europeans who regard Russia as a threat to their homeland went up from 29 per cent in 1992 to 39 per cent in 1996. On the other hand, 61 per cent of all Eastern European respondents think that Russia poses no threat to their country. The second international danger for those countries of the former Warsaw Pact are the neighbouring countries. In 1992, 49 per cent of all post-Communist citizens were afraid of some of their neighbours; this proportion went down in the

Table 7.1 Subjective perceptions of threat in post-Communist Europe

Q. Do you think any of these factors poses a threat or no threat to peace and security in this society? (= big threat + some threat)

	NDB 2 *1992*	*NDB 4* *1996*	*NDB 5* *1998*	*Change* *1992–8*
Minorities, ethnic groups	(2)	(3)	(1)	
Threat	40	25	29	−11
Immigrants, refugees	(3)	(4)	(2)	
Threat	36	22	26	−10
Russia	(4)	(1)	(3)	
Threat	29	39	24	−5
Neighbouring countries	(1)	(2)	(4)	
Threat	49	28	23	−26
Germany	(5)	(5)	(5)	
Threat	19	20	21	+2
USA	(6)	(6)	(6)	
Threat	8	14	21	+13

Sources: New Democracies Barometer 2 (= NDB 2) 1992; N = 10.518. New Democracies Barometer 4 (= NDB 4) 1996; N = 10.441. New Democracies Barometer 5 (= NDB 5) 1998; N = 11.296. Total number of face-to-face interviews: N = 32.255.

following six years to 28 per cent in 1996. One can assume that roughly one-third of Eastern Europeans are afraid of some neighbouring states although the subjective threat by one's neighbours decreased from one-half to one-third over time. In 1996, 72 per cent of post-Communist citizens believed that their neighbours no longer posed a military threat to them. This may be because most of the borders between and around post-Communist countries have now been confirmed through international treaties, thus reducing the possibility of dispute over territory. However, a number of disputed borders and territories in the region also remain unresolved.

The third strongest danger for this part of the world are minorities and ethnic groups within the country. In 1992, 40 per cent of all East Europeans felt threatened by minorities and ethnic groups inside their own country, but that number fell to 25 per cent in 1996. As with neighbouring states, the fear of instability caused by ethnic groups within the country cooled down in the first half of the 1990s considerably. In 1996, 75 per cent of all post-Communist citizens expressed no anxieties about ethnic groups or minorities threatening the internal peace and stability of their own country. A similar longitudinal pattern appears with regard to threat from immigrants and refugees. In 1992, 36 per cent of all East Europeans were quite nervous about migrants 'flooding' their country and thus producing political and social instability, but that share went down to 22 per cent in 1996, which is still quite high, but the trend is definitely downwards during the observed period.

The 'German threat' and the 'American threat' are much lower compared with the Russian Federation, the neighbouring states, internal minorities or external migrants, but nevertheless we can speak of some individual or group anxiety about potential actions by Germany or the United States of America. One-fifth of all post-Communist citizens regard Germany as a threat to their country, a percentage that is constant over time. On the other hand, 80 per cent of all Eastern Europeans do not see any danger arising from Germany's ambitions towards the East. In 1992, only 8 per cent associated some danger with the USA, but that share increased to 15 per cent in 1996. Over time, more Eastern Europeans feel threatened by US foreign policy.

In an overview of the subjective perceptions of military threat one might argue that, on the one hand, the fear of threat by 'great powers' – Germany, America and especially Russia – had grown between 1992 and 1996. There could be a growing strategic cleavage in Central and Eastern Europe, at least in the mind of the post-Communist peoples in the region. On the other hand, the anxieties concerning destabilising effects caused by neighbouring countries, by internal minorities or external migrants lost their impact upon the ordinary citizens in Eastern Europe and are recently less pressing than in 1992. Next we will turn to more detailed analyses of who is afraid of Russia, Germany and America.

Who is afraid of Russia?

The leading group with extremely high levels of military distrust about the Russian Federation and their future strategic intentions is Croatia and Poland. The feeling of being threatened by the Russian Federation is highest in Croatia (see Table 7.2). In 1992, 33 per cent of the Croatian population expressed some anxiety about the Russian Federation and their strategic intentions. That share increased tremendously over time and reached the level of 71 per cent of Croatians in 1996. One explanation for this steep increase could be the open support of the Russian Federation for the Federal Republic of Yugoslavia during the war in Bosnia.

The other nation which also feels threatened by Russia is Poland. The high level of Polish mistrust about the Russian military potential was constant over time with 66 per cent of the Polish population expressing fear

Table 7.2 Perceived threat by the Russian Federation

Q. Do you think Russia poses a threat to peace and security in this society?
(= big threat + some threat)

	NDB 2 *1992*	*NDB 4* *1996*	*NDB 5* *1998*	*Change* *1992–8*
Poland	(1)	(1)	(1)	
Threat	66	71	62	−4
Czech Republic	(3)	(3)	(2)	
Threat	39	55	48	+9
Slovakia	(5)	(5)	(3)	
Threat	26	51	45	+19
Romania	(2)	(4)	(4)	
Threat	62	55	42	−20
Croatia	(4)	(2)	(5)	
Threat	33	71	18	−15
Ukraine	(6)	(8)	(6)	
Threat	20	17	14	−6
Hungary	(7)	(6)	(7)	
Threat	13	30	13	0
Belarus	(8)	(9)	(8)	
Threat	13	15	13	0
FR of Yugoslavia	*	*	(9)	
Threat	*	*	11	
Bulgaria	(9)	(10)	(10)	
Threat	6	5	6	0
Slovenia	(10)	(7)	(11)	
Threat	3	21	3	0

Sources: New Democracies Barometer 2 (= NDB 2) 1992; N = 10.518. New Democracies Barometer 4 (= NDB 4) 1996; N = 10.441. New Democracies Barometer 5 (= NDB 5) 1998; N = 11.296. Total number of face-to-face interviews: N = 32.255.

Note
*Not done in this country at this time.

about Russia in 1992, and 71 per cent of the Poles with the same feeling of Russian threat in 1996. Only one-third of the Polish people do not feel threatened by their Eastern neighbour, Russia.

The second group of post-Communist countries with high levels of military distrust about future Russian intentions are the Czech Republic, Romania and Slovakia. In 1992, 39 per cent of the Czech population felt threatened by Russia, a share which increased quite considerably to 55 per cent in 1996. In Romania, 62 per cent of the Romanian respondents expressed some anxiety about perceived Russian military intentions in 1992. This Romanian fear of future Russian military activities decreased to 55 per cent in 1996, hence displaying now the same level of military distrust towards the Russian Federation as the Czech Republic. In Slovakia, the scepticism of the Slovakian general public about future Russian military strategies grew considerably over time. In 1992, 26 per cent of the population felt threatened by Russia, a share which increased to 51 per cent in 1996. Therefore we cannot speak of increasing friendship and closeness between Slovakia and the Russian Federation in security terms, at least not at the level of the ordinary citizens in Slovakia.

Romanians also feel threatened by Russia and this could be on account of the military interventions of the Soviet/Russian Fourteenth Army in 1992 in the neighbouring Transnistria province of Moldova, which is ethnically similar to Romania and was formerly a part of Romania. By 1996, hostilities there had ceased. It could also be a legacy of the anti-Russian stance of the Ceauşescu regime.

In Hungary, the feeling of military threat by Russia grew over time too. In 1992, only 13 per cent of Hungarians felt threatened by Russia. This changed in the first half of the 1990s with the effect that 30 per cent of the Hungarian population was quite concerned about the 'Russian danger' in 1996. The extent of military distrust concerning Russia increased sharply in Slovenia. In 1992, only 3 per cent of the Slovenian population was afraid of the Russians, whereas more than one-fifth of the Slovenes (21 per cent) felt threatened by Russia in 1996. As with Croatia, the high level of military distrust in Slovenia seems to be linked to the Russian military and political affiliation with the Federal Republic of Yugoslavia in general and Serbian nationality in particular.

However, it is also rather surprising that fear of Russia actually grew in most of the Central European countries, since they do not have direct borders with Russia (except in the case of Poland) and since the Soviet troops had all left by 1996. In the countries which have direct borders with Russia and towards which Russia was making various claims, there was much less fear of their traditionally dominant Eastern neighbour.

The situation in the post-Soviet countries such as Belarus and the Ukraine is, as along many other attitudinal dimensions, quite different. In the Ukraine, only 17 per cent of the Ukrainian population was nervous about the Russian military in 1996. A similar picture emerges in Belarus, where 15 per cent expressed some anxiety about future Russian military intentions. The level of a perceived Russian military threat in both former Soviet Republics is constant over time. Bulgaria is strikingly free of any feeling of threat from Russia: 5 per cent of the Bulgarians feel threatened by Russia, whereas 95 per cent of the Bulgarian population show no military nervousness about the Russian Federation whatsoever. As in many other attitudes in post-Communist Europe, a high level of homogeneity can be noticed between the post-Soviet countries Belarus and the Ukraine on the one hand, and Bulgaria on the other.

Analysis of different levels of trust and distrust concerning the military strategy of the Russian Federation in the future showed that the countries which were in the process of joining NATO in 1997 also have quite high levels of military distrust about Russian military intentions: Poland, the Czech Republic and Hungary. The top position of Croatia in the anti-Russian league can be explained by the war situation in the territory of former Yugoslavia; in that respect, Croatia, Bosnia and the Federal Republic of Yugoslavia are still 'societies at war' and cannot be compared fully with other post-Communist societies in transformation. In terms of the subjective feeling of threat by the general population, Romania would also qualify as member of NATO, a view that was evidently shared by some European countries, but not by the USA. The military climate of the Slovakian population is in stark contrast to the images of pro-Russian feelings in Slovakia, which are frequently presented in the Western press, but are definitely wrong in that aspect of international integration.

With regard to perceptions of threat from Russia, there was therefore a division among the countries under consideration. Some feared Russia and their fear was growing, but these were the countries with the greatest geographical distance from Russia. Other countries did not fear Russia and their fear was even decreasing – these were the countries closest geographically, linguistically and politically to Russia.

Who is afraid of Germany?

The perceived threat by Germany is constant over time: one-fifth of the Eastern European population think that Germany poses a threat to peace and security to their home country (20 per cent in 1996); however, different countries feared Germany at different periods. The highest level of anti-German feelings in strategic terms is visible in two neighbouring states to Germany, Poland and the Czech Republic. In 1996, 45 per cent of the Polish population and 44 per cent of the Czech population felt threatened by Germany (see Table 7.3). Poland and the Czech Republic display the same level of anti-German feelings, but this is a result of divergent trends. In Poland we had an extremely high level of public distrust towards Germany in 1992, when 70 per cent of the Polish population expressed fears about the potential military intentions of Germany. The

Table 7.3 Perceived threat from Germany

Q. Do you think Germany poses a threat or no threat to peace and security in this society? (= big threat + some threat)

	NDB 2 1992	NDB 4 1996	NDB 5 1998	Change 1992–8
FR of Yugoslavia	*	*	(1)	
Threat	*	*	75	*
Poland	(1)	(1)	(2)	
Threat	70	45	42	−28
Czech Republic	(2)	(2)	(3)	
Threat	38	44	37	−1
Slovakia	(3)	(3)	(4)	
Threat	21	32	23	+2
Belarus	(4)	(5)	(5)	
Threat	15	21	15	0
Romania	(5)	(6)	(6)	
Threat	13	15	14	+1
Ukraine	(7)	(7)	(7)	
Threat	3	12	11	+8
Croatia	(8)	(4)	(8)	
Threat	3	23	6	+3
Hungary	(6)	(8)	(9)	
Threat	7	5	3	−4
Slovenia	(9)	(9)	(10)	
Threat	3	5	3	0
Bulgaria	(10)	(10)	(11)	
Threat	3	3	2	−1

Sources: New Democracies Barometer 2 (= NDB 2) 1992; N = 10.518. New Democracies Barometer 4 (= NDB 4) 1996; N = 10.441. New Democracies Barometer 5 (= NDB 5) 1998; N = 11.296. Total number of face-to-face interviews: N = 32.255.

Note
*Not done in this country at this time.

enormous amount of anti-German feelings went down in the course of the first half of the 1990s to 45 per cent, which is still considerable and not to be underestimated. Hence, we are entitled to speak of an erosion of anti-German feelings in Poland by 25 percentage points, but in the Czech Republic the trend is reversed. In 1992, 38 per cent of the Czech general public distrusted Germany concerning her strategic intentions, a figure which went up to 44 per cent in 1996. Thus, we notice a rise of anti-German feelings from a military–strategic point of view in the Czech Republic by 6 percentage points between the beginning and the middle of the 1990s.

As in the Czech Republic, anti-German sentiments concerning the military dimension are rising in Slovakia too. In 1992, 21 per cent of the Slovakian population thought that Germany posed a threat to Slovakia, which increased to 32 per cent in 1996. Hence, we can argue that one-third of Slovakian society has serious concerns about the 'German danger' in 1996. A similar pattern is visible in Croatia, but on a lower general level. In 1992, only 3 per cent of the Croatian population were afraid of Germany. This coincided with the strong German and Austrian diplomatic support for Croatian independence during that period, which was seen very favourably by the Croatian public. In 1996, however, the picture had changed considerably. At the later time we find 23 per cent of the Croatian sample expressing fears about the military potential of Germany, maybe in relation to the peace-keeping and peace-enforcing operations in that region, which involved German combat troops for the first time ever since the end of the Second World War. There was a 20 percentage point rise in Croatian anti-German feelings, which is quite remarkable in comparison with other countries. The military threat of Germany is also more visible in Belarus, where 21 per cent feel a certain military threat arising from Germany in 1996.

In Romania, one can see 15 per cent of the population concerned about the German military power in 1996, which is constant over time. The perception of German military potential grew in the Ukraine from 3 per cent in 1992 to 12 per cent in 1996, whereas the Hungarians display no clear fear of German military power: only 5 per cent of the Hungarian population think that Germany poses a threat to Hungary, which is negligible. The same goes for Slovenia, where 5 per cent associate some danger with the German military potential. Finally, in Bulgaria we do not find any anti-German feelings from the military point of view at all.

In general, fewer people feared Germany than feared Russia, but this fear was growing among some countries. Some of those countries that most feared Russia also feared Germany; for them the neighbouring 'great powers' were a threat.

Who is afraid of America?

The perception of military threat exerted by the USA is the lowest of all security risks within Central and Eastern Europe. Nevertheless, the percentage of Eastern Europeans concerned about the military power of the USA grew from 8 per cent in 1992 to 15 per cent in 1996 (see Table 7.4). As a consequence of the military events in the territory of former Yugoslavia in the first half of the 1990s, Croatia displays the highest level of military distrust concerning the USA. In 1992, only 8 per cent of the Croatian population felt the USA was a threat to the Croatian state, whereas we find 29 per cent of the adult Croatian population in 1996 are anxious about the American military power and its possible effects upon Croatia and its geopolitical position. In Belarus, the anti-American feelings increased from 13 per cent in 1992 to 24 per cent in 1996. Recently, one-quarter of the Byelorussians think that the USA is a real danger for

Table 7.4 Perceived threat from the USA

Q. Do you think the USA poses a threat to peace and security in this society?
(= big threat + some threat)

	NDB 2 1992	NDB 4 1996	NDB 5 1998	Change 1992–8
FR of Yugoslavia	*	*	(1)	
Threat	*	*	85	*
Belarus	(2)	(2)	(2)	
Threat	13	24	26	+13
Slovakia	(7)	(3)	(3)	
Threat	5	22	24	+19
Ukraine	(8)	(4)	(4)	
Threat	4	16	21	+17
Czech Republic	(6)	(5)	(5)	
Threat	6	14	16	+10
Poland	(3)	(8)	(6)	
Threat	11	8	15	+4
Romania	(4)	(6)	(7)	
Threat	10	14	13	+3
Croatia	(5)	(1)	(8)	
Threat	8	29	12	+4
Bulgaria	(9)	(7)	(9)	
Threat	4	9	7	+3
Hungary	(10)	(9)	(10)	
Threat	3	5	4	+1
Slovenia	(1)	(10)	(11)	
Threat	14	5	4	−10

Sources: New Democracies Barometer 2 (= NDB 2) 1992; N = 10.518. New Democracies Barometer 4 (= NDB 4) 1996; N = 10.441. New Democracies Barometer 5 (= NDB 5) 1998; N = 11.296. Total number of face-to-face interviews: N = 32.255.

Note
*Not done in this country at this time.

Belarus, a phenomenon that could be linked eventually to the close strategic alliance between the Russian Federation and Belarus in the last two years. In Slovakia, one noticed a considerable rise in anti-American feelings since the early 1990s. In 1992, only 5 per cent of the Slovakian population felt threatened by the USA, but that figure increased to 22 per cent in 1996. Now, more than one-fifth of the Slovakian population is concerned about the American military potential and its possible effects upon Slovakian security. This change in the Slovakian public mood could be an outcome of domestic Slovakian politics and the basic ideological orientations of the current political regime in Bratislava. In the Ukraine we find a similar development as in Belarus, a very low level of anti-American sentiments at the beginning of the transformation process (4 per cent in 1992) and a steep increase of up to 16 per cent of Ukrainians nervous about American military power in 1996.

In four of the countries under consideration, roughly one-tenth of the population displays some fears about the military power of the USA. These are the Czech Republic, Romania, Bulgaria and Poland. The vast majority of people in those countries – around 90 per cent – are not afraid of America or American military potential. Nevertheless, one should note that the very low level of anti-American feelings in those four countries is growing steadily to higher levels, a trend which should be observed in the future. In Hungary and Slovenia, virtually nobody is afraid of the Americans. Therefore, in most countries fear of the USA had also grown, although it remains at far lower levels than fear of either Russia or Germany.

Who is afraid of neighbouring countries?

The second biggest military threat after Russia comes from the respective neighbouring states. However, an important finding is that the immediate threat at the borders seems to be less strong and frightening than at the beginning of the 1990s (see Table 7.5).

Again, the situation in the territory of former Yugoslavia is very different and undoubtedly influenced by the armed conflicts following the dissolution of Yugoslavia. The absolute majority of Slovenes (60 per cent) and of Croatians (55 per cent) are afraid of the Serbians in Bosnia-Herzegovina and of the Federal Republic of Yugoslavia. That subjective perception of a Serbian threat has decreased only slightly since 1992.

The country occupying third place among those most threatened by their neighbours is Hungary. In 1992, 64 per cent of the Hungarian population felt threatened by their neighbours. This Hungarian strategic 'complex' concerning her neighbours cooled down to 48 per cent in 1996. Nevertheless, we can still see that the Hungarian population is afraid of their neighbours. This could be an outcome of the proximity of Hungary to the armed conflicts taking place in the former Yugoslavia and the large number of refugees who fled across the border into Hungary. It is also the case that Hungarian ethnic minorities live over the border in most directions and this could give Hungarians a special sensitivity to the situation in their neighbouring countries. Most notably, there has been some tension between the Romanian government and the Hungarian minority who are living there and the same is the case for Slovakia.

A similar picture of strategic landscapes appears in Slovakia, which happens to be a neighbour of Hungary with a considerable Hungarian minority in Southern Slovakia. In 1992, 46 per cent of the Slovakian general public felt threatened by their neighbours. That share of ordinary Slovakians nervous about potential military activities in the neighbourhood decreased to 36 per cent in 1996, which is still clearly more than one-third of the adult Slovakian population. Domestic politicians and proposals, for example by Meciar, for a population exchange with Hungary

Table 7.5 Perceived threat from neighbouring countries

Q. Do you think the neighbouring countries pose a threat to peace and security in this society? (= big threat + some threat)

	NDB 2 1992	NDB 4 1996	NDB 5 1998	Change 1992–8
FR of Yugoslavia	*	*	(1)	*
Threat	*	*	59	*
Croatia	(4)	(1)	(2)	*
Threat	62	55	31	−31
Slovakia	(7)	(3)	(3)	*
Threat	46	36	30	−16
Romania	(1)	(4)	(4)	*
Threat	67	35	27	−40
Hungary	(2)	(2)	(5)	*
Threat	64	48	23	−41
Poland	(3)	(6)	(6)	*
Threat	63	15	20	−43
Bulgaria	(5)	(5)	(7)	*
Threat	61	31	19	−42
Belarus	(9)	(8)	(8)	*
Threat	20	11	13	−7
Slovenia	(6)	*	(9)	*
Threat	60	*	11	−49
Czech Republic	(8)	(7)	(10)	*
Threat	36	14	8	−28
Ukraine	(10)	(9)	(11)	*
Threat	11	9	8	−3

Sources: New Democracies Barometer 2 (= NDB 2) 1992; = 10.518. New Democracies Barometer 4 (= NDB 4) 1996; N = 10.441. New Democracies Barometer 5 (= NDB 5) 1998; N = 11.296. Total number of face-to-face interviews: N = 32.255.

Note
* Not done in this country at this time.

of ethnic Hungarians and Slovaks, exacerbate this mood of threat in Slovakia.

In Romania, the general feeling of threat by the neighbouring states decreased during the 1990s. In 1992, a majority of 67 per cent of Romanians felt threatened by their neighbours, whereas this was only 35 per cent in 1996. This change could be because of the military tensions in Moldova in the early 1990s, which have since disappeared and the greater harmonisation of relations with Hungary. Despite this obvious growth in Romanian confidence, we can see that there are still more than one-third of Romanian women and men who felt some threat from neighbouring states.

We found also a high level of military distrust towards neighbouring states in Bulgaria. In 1992, 61 per cent of the Bulgarians expressed their doubts about the peaceful intentions of the neighbours, thus displaying a high degree of nervousness about their immediate neighbourhood. The widespread strategic anxiety within the Bulgarian general public at the beginning of the 1990s calmed down in the following years with the effect that we find only less than one-third of Bulgarians (31 per cent) who are still anxious about the military intentions of their neighbouring states in 1996. The war in Yugoslavia, taking place just over the Bulgarian border, and its cessation may have affected these attitudes.

A very low level of military anxiety can be found in Poland (15 per cent), the Czech Republic (14 per cent), Belarus (11 per cent) and the Ukraine (9 per cent). The stabilisation of the military thinking of the population is quite remarkable in Poland, where 63 per cent felt threatened by the Polish neighbours in 1992 – one could speak of high level of alertness on the brink of being alarmed. The relative strategic stabilisation in the Baltic countries, Belarus and the Ukraine in the period between 1992 and 1996 perhaps had a calming effect on the Polish populace. A similar, but less dramatic, development occurred in the Czech Republic. In 1992, 36 per cent of the Czech population were afraid of their neighbours. That share decreased during the first half of the 1990s to 14 per cent, which showed that the Czech general public became more and more relaxed about the perceived military intentions of their neighbours. One interpretation of the high level of military confidence and a corresponding low level of military anxiety about neighbouring states in Belarus could be that the strategic closeness of Belarus to Russia produced a feeling of territorial security in that former Soviet Republic.

Internal threats: who is afraid of ethnic groups and minorities?

If one analyses the perceived threat exerted by ethnic groups and minorities to internal stability and security across Eastern Europe, the first outcome is that ethnic tensions in that region seem to have calmed down somewhat, at least in most of the countries. The average for all NDB countries went down from 40 per cent feeling threatened in 1992 to 25 per cent under subjective threat in 1996, which leaves nevertheless one-quarter of all Eastern Europeans who think that their internal security is threatened by ethnic minorities in their country (see Table 7.6).

The country with the highest level of ethnic tensions appears to be Slovakia. One half of the Slovakian population (48 per cent in 1996) is under the impression that ethnic minorities pose a threat to peace and security in Slovakia. That share of Slovakians concerned about ethnic groups remained constant over time. This is perhaps the consequence of the on-going problems with the Hungarian minority of about 500,000 on the southern border who want the use of their own language in the region in opposition to the policies of the Slovak government. The second highest level of subjective ethnic threat can be found in Croatia. In 1992, about 57 per cent of the Croatian population felt threatened by ethnic

Table 7.6 Perceived threat from ethnic groups and minorities

Q. Do you think that ethnic groups and minorities within our country pose a threat to peace and security in this society? (= big threat + some threat)

	NDB 2 *1992*	*NDB 4* *1996*	*NDB 5* *1998*	*Change* *1992–8*
FR of Yugoslavia	*	*	(1)	
Threat	*	*	70	*
Slovakia	(3)	(1)	(2)	
Threat	53	48	43	−10
Croatia	(2)	(2)	(3)	
Threat	57	40	39	−18
Romania	(1)	(4)	(4)	
Threat	60	32	32	−28
Bulgaria	(4)	(3)	(5)	
Threat	46	37	29	−17
Czech Republic	(5)	(6)	(6)	
Threat	44	15	24	−20
Hungary	(8)	(7)	(7)	
Threat	26	15	19	−7
Poland	(6)	(10)	(8)	
Threat	37	8	18	−19
Ukraine	(9)	(8)	(9)	
Threat	25	14	15	−10
Belarus	(7)	(9)	(10)	
Threat	30	14	14	−16
Slovenia	(10)	(5)	(11)	
Threat	14	20	10	−4

Sources: New Democracies Barometer 2 (= NDB 2) 1992; N = 10.518. New Democracies Barometer 4 (= NDB 4) 1996; N = 10.441. New Democracies Barometer 5 (= NDB 5) 1998; N = 11.296. Total number of face-to-face interviews: N = 32.255.

Note
* Not done in this country at this time.

minorities, especially Serbs and other ethnic groups on the other side of the war. That percentage went down to 40 per cent in 1996, but must be regarded still as quite high by comparison with other post-Communist societies. Croatia seems to be still a society at war, but the first signs of normalisation are visible. The subjective level of ethnic threat is also quite high in Bulgaria with the unsolved Turkish question and in Romania with strong Hungarian minorities in Western Romania. These are all countries with what might be termed 'dominant minorities'. Those countries whose populations contain 'dominant minorities' are the ones with the strongest perception of internal insecurity from this source.

Slovenia is the only country where the level of subjective ethnic distrust went up between 1992 and 1996 from 14 per cent to 20 per cent, albeit at a quite low general level. In the remaining countries such as the Czech Republic, Hungary, Belarus, the Ukraine and Poland, the level of ethnic threats within societies from minorities towards the majorities decreased considerably. In the Czech Republic we witness a fall from 44 per cent Czechs feeling threatened by Czech ethnic groups in 1992 to 15 per cent in 1996. Much of this is because of the separation from Slovakia, where most of the ethnic minorities in the former Czechoslovakia were living. In Hungary, the downward tendency is not as steep as in the Czech Republic: 26 per cent of Hungarians felt threatened by ethnic groups in 1992, compared to only 15 per cent of the Hungarian population in 1996.

In Belarus and the Ukraine the attitudinal pattern of anxieties about ethnic groups producing internal insecurity is again similar: in both countries 14 per cent feel threatened by ethnic minorities in 1996. In both post-Soviet countries the level of subjective ethnic tensions within the general public has fallen considerably since 1992. An interesting outcome of that analysis is that Poland is the post-Communist country with the lowest levels of subjective ethnic insecurity in 1996. The anxiety about minorities endangering the peace and stability of Polish society was at 37 per cent quite high in 1992. Since then, we seem to observe a definite cooling down of ethnic tensions in Poland. If this is a stable trend, we will be able to decide only by measuring the same phenomenon in future New Democracies Barometers.

Internal threats: who is afraid of migrants and refugees?

An interesting question in the panorama of potential or real threats to Eastern European societies is the perception of migrants moving between different countries, especially between what we have described as the Central European buffer zone (Poland, the Czech Republic, Slovakia, Hungary and Slovenia) and Western Europe, on the one hand, and between the buffer zone and Eastern Europe on the other. The threat by migrants was expressed by 36 per cent of all Eastern Europeans in 1992, but went down to 22 per cent in 1996. As in the case of ethnic minorities within post-Communist societies, the fear of migrants as a threat to the peace and security of the country decreased from one-third to one-fifth of the Eastern European general public (see Table 7.7).

The highest level of concern about migrants and refugees can be found in Croatia with the special problem of war refugees from Bosnia-Herzegovina escaping to Croatia, Slovenia, Austria and Germany. The re-migration process from Germany and Austria has started, but necessarily puts additional demographic pressure upon Slovenia and Croatia. In 1992, 59 per cent of all Croatians felt threatened by migrants from other parts of the former Yugoslavia. This figure fell to 34 per cent in 1996, which is still the highest value over all Central and Eastern Europe. The second highest level of anxieties about migrants was found in Hungary, one of the main 'buffer zone' countries. The perceived threat by migrants for Hungary went down from 51 per cent of the population concerned in

Table 7.7 Perceived threat from immigrants and refugees

Q. Do you think immigrants and refugees from other societies pose a threat or
no threat to peace and security to this country?' (= big threat + some threat)

	NDB 2 1992	NDB 4 1996	NDB 5 1998	Change 1992–8
Slovakia	(6)	(3)	(1)	
Threat	23	28	40	+17
Czech Republic	(5)	(4)	(2)	
Threat	38	26	38	0
Hungary	(3)	(2)	(3)	
Threat	51	33	35	−16
Croatia	(2)	(1)	(4)	
Threat	59	34	33	−26
FR of Yugoslavia	*	*	(5)	
Threat	*	*	25	*
Poland	(4)	(7)	(6)	
Threat	41	14	24	−17
Belarus	(7)	(6)	(7)	
Threat	22	19	22	0
Romania	(8)	(8)	(8)	
Threat	16	13	22	+6
Slovenia	(1)	(5)	(9)	
Threat	61	25	16	−45
Ukraine	(9)	(10)	(10)	
Threat	6	12	15	+9
Bulgaria		(9)	(11)	
Threat	*	13	14	+1

Sources: New Democracies Barometer 2 (= NDB 2) 1992; N = 10.518. New Democracies
Barometer 4 (= NDB 4) 1996; N = 10.441. New Democracies Barometer 5 (= NDB 5) 1998;
N = 11.296. Total number of face-to-face interviews: N = 32.255.

Note
* Not done in this country at this time.

1992 to 33 per cent of the Hungarian public in 1996. Hungary was also
the country which received the most refugees from the former Yugoslavia
of all the countries outside of the former Yugoslavia itself (Fullerton *et al.*
1995).

Slovakia is one of the only countries, together with the Ukraine, where
the anxiety about incoming migrants and refugees has grown over time.
In 1992, 23 per cent of the Slovakians felt threatened by migrants; this
figure rose to 28 per cent in 1996, putting Slovakia in the third position in
the scale of anxiety about migrants. This is surprising, since Slovakia
receives relatively few migrants compared with her neighbours (Wallace *et
al.* 1997), but may reflect the rising xenophobic rhetoric of the political
leaders during the regime of Vladimir Meciar. Originally, the aversion
against migrants was much higher in the Czech Republic than in Slovakia,
but anti-migrant feeling went down from 38 per cent in 1992 to 26 per

cent in 1996, falling below the Slovakian level of anti-migrant feelings within the population. Slovenia was in 1992 in a completely different position due to the war and the massive flows of migrants and war refugees following the collapse of Yugoslavia. The substantial migration between Slovenia, Croatia, Bosnia-Herzegovina and the other former Republics of Yugoslavia in 1992 produced the result that 61 per cent of the Slovenian society felt threatened by migrants and refugees. This was a real and not an imagined danger within Slovenia, but also in Croatia.

In Belarus, the fear of migrants is well below the NDB average and with one-fifth of the Byelorussian society constant over time. In 1996, 19 per cent of the Byelorussian sample indicates that they feel threatened by migrants and refugees. In Poland we encounter again the process of 'normalisation': in 1992, 41 per cent of the Polish population were quite concerned about the migration pressure, whereas only 14 per cent of the Polish general public were still nervous about migrants and refugees threatening peace and order in Polish society in 1996. In Bulgaria, Romania and the Ukraine we find similarly low levels of a perceived threat by migrants as in Poland with values around 13 per cent, whereas 90 per cent in those four countries are quite relaxed about migrants. One explanation for that outcome could be that these countries are the ones sending rather than receiving migrants.

Subjective insecurity index

Putting together all these sources of insecurity, we developed an index in order to measure how insecure in general each country was feeling. The index was constructed by assigning a score of 1 to those countries who ranked tenth in the list of countries on one dimension, a score of 2 to the country ranking ninth and so on, so that those ranking first received a score of 10. There were six dimensions: fear of neighbouring states; fear of internal minorities and ethnic groups; fear of refugees and migrants; fear of Germany, Russia and USA. The score for each country was then added together to give a measurement of how insecure each country felt overall. The maximum score was 60 and the minimum score 6. The results are presented in Table 7.8. The subjective threat index shows that Croatia is the most insecure country in terms of the anxieties of the population. Out of a maximum value of 60, Croatia scored 55, which means that it was the most subjectively insecure country in nearly all of the fields we have been discussing. On account of the war, the people of Croatia feel threatened from all directions – from neighbouring countries, from great powers, and from internal insecurity engendered by migrants and minorities.

The second most anxious country was Slovakia, which also rated highly on both internal and external security threats. During the era of Prime Minister Meciar, the political isolation of Slovakia from the other Central

Table 7.8 Ranking of most threatened countries

	Threat–Index	Russia	Neighbouring states	Internal minorities and ethnic groups	External migrants and refugees	Germany	USA
Maximum value:	60						
Croatia	55	1	2	2	1	4	1
Slovakia	47	5	4	1	3	3	3
Czech Republic	38	3	8	6	4	2	5
Romania	32	4	5	4	9	6	6
Poland	31	2	7	10	7	1	8
Hungary	31	6	3	7	2	8	9
Slovenia	29	7	1	5	5	9	10
Belarus	27	9	9	8	6	5	2
Bulgaria	22	10	6	3	8	10	7
Ukraine	18	8	10	9	10	7	4

Note
Basis = ranks in six fields of threat.

European countries (its exclusion from membership discussions for NATO and for the European Union, as well as repeated warnings from the Council of Europe and from the European Commission with regard to various positions taken by the Slovak government) perhaps created or exacerbated this sense of threat. Furthermore, the xenophobic and often aggressive rhetoric of the Meciar government may have had some effect in generating an insecure atmosphere.

The third most anxious country in terms of subjective insecurity was the Czech Republic. It is mainly the people's fear of great powers – Russia and Germany – which put the Czech Republic in this position.

Romania, Poland, Hungary and Slovenia are all clustered together with between 32 and 29 points each. In the case of Romania, Poland and Slovenia, there have been significant reductions in anxiety about military threat or internal destabilisation in recent years.

The final cluster of countries are the former Soviet states of the Ukraine and Belarus and the country most sympathetic to them – Bulgaria. What is surprising is that this group of countries which have perhaps the most to fear from internal and external insecurity (Bulgaria has a continuing unresolved problem with its Turkish and Muslim minorities) and who appear to be the most fragile and most recently constructed democracies are in fact the least worried about military insecurity. These are the least well-established democracies but also the least fearful.

Attitudes toward military integration into NATO

The feeling of insecurity may lead some post-Communist countries to a desire to join NATO in order to secure their military position as part of a greater alliance (see Table 7.9). The fear of Russia may also make joining NATO a desirable objective. In general, a very high percentage of the population of post-Communist East and Central Europe wished to join NATO. On average 64 per cent – nearly two-thirds – of all the people combined saw joining NATO as beneficial. This rose to 90 per cent in Romania and 86 per cent in Slovenia and Poland. Croatia followed with three-quarters of her population – 76 per cent – having this opinion. The Czech Republic, Slovakia and Hungary were clustered together with around two-thirds in favour of joining NATO.

We can see that in general those countries that felt the least subjective insecurity – the Ukraine, Bulgaria and Belarus – were also the ones least likely to want to join NATO. Belarus was the only country with a majority – two-thirds (69 per cent) – *against* joining NATO. Nevertheless, one-third of Bulgarians and Byelorussians and more than one half of Ukrainians expressed a desire to join NATO. While in all countries opinions were polarised between those who were for joining NATO and those who were against, in Bulgaria there was a very high number of 'don't knows' – 39 per cent. Perhaps this reflects the uncertainty in Bulgaria as to whether the country should be looking westwards or eastwards in its strategic alliances.

These results are corroborated by those of the United States Information Agency (USIA), which carries out regular surveys on security issues in these countries (USIA 1997). Of people who said that they strongly favour or favour becoming a full member of NATO, they found Romanians (79 per cent) were among the highest scorers followed by Slovenia with 71 per

Table 7.9 Perception of NATO membership

Statement: Membership in NATO is a good thing (very good + good)

	NDB 4 *1996*	*NDB 5* *1998*	*Change* *1996–8*
Croatia	76	74	−2
Poland	86	73	−13
Slovenia	86	69	−17
Hungary	62	68	+6
Czech Republic	63	67	+4
Romania	90	62	−28
Slovakia	62	60	−2
Bulgaria	34	53	+19
FR of Yugoslavia	*	50	*
Ukraine	58	45	−13
Belarus	31	36	+5

cent and Poland with 72 per cent. Next came Hungary (57 per cent), Bulgaria (52 per cent), the Czech Republic (51 per cent) and Slovakia (46 per cent). This survey was also carried out in 1996 but did not include the former Soviet Republics of the Ukraine and Belarus. They conclude that support for joining NATO is shallow and has declined since 1995. However, we would disagree with this conclusion. It seems to us that support is not shallow – it is very high and continues to be high despite some decline since 1996. More than half of most of the countries questioned wanted to become full members of NATO. However, USIA found that even if Central and Eastern European countries are keen to join NATO, they are not keen to assume the responsibilities of NATO membership including routine exercises in their country, having NATO troops stationed in their country, having regular over-flights from NATO aircraft or sending troops to support another NATO ally. Furthermore, the large majority in each country favour social over military spending.

Ironically, those countries that most desired to join NATO – Slovenia and Romania – are not the countries which have been accepted into the alliance. Although Bulgaria is to a great extent eastwards-looking or ambivalent about its directions, neighbouring Romania is emphatically westwards-looking. This is borne out in other indicators of economic and political orientation as well (Wallace 1997). Hungary and the Czech Republic, who have been accepted into the alliance, are not as enthusiastic about it as some of the other countries, falling below the mean for the whole group. The people of Poland, on the other hand, should feel pleased that they have been allowed to join – they are also very enthusiastic about it.

The results imply that the countries of the Central European buffer zone feel far more insecurity than the countries of the former Soviet Union in our sample, and these are also the countries which would most like to join NATO.

In general, we can see that in the post-Communist Central European countries the sense of threat from internal problems – migrants and ethnic minorities – has generally gone down since 1996. The same goes for feelings of threat from neighbouring states. The exceptions to this rule would be the countries affected by the recent war among the states that make up the former Yugoslavia. However, a sense of threat from the great powers has increased, most notably any threat by Russia and Germany, followed by the USA.

What is also noticeable is that the region divides into distinct blocs. The former Soviet states have far less fear and anxiety than do the buffer zone states of Hungary, Poland, the Czech and Slovak Republics. High anxiety can also be found among Romanians and Slovenians. These are the countries most eager to join the European Union and NATO. They are also the countries which have 'westernised' most in their economic and political reforms. They presumably feel themselves to be part of a western bloc. By contrast, Belarus, the Ukraine and Bulgaria feel themselves to be more part of an Eastern bloc of countries. Croatia is in rather an untypical situation being a recent participant in war and people in Croatia are the most insecure in the region, although this insecurity has declined somewhat since 1992.

Those feeling threatened can be subdivided into distinct groups. First, there are those who feel threatened by both internal and external factors, but their anxiety is not associated with anything else except anxiety. They are a very insecure group. The second group see only external powers or countries as a threat to peace and security. The third group see only Russia as being the problem and these were divided between lower educated men who were also economically insecure and higher educated people who were economically secure. Economic insecurity does not therefore directly lead to any sense of insecurity or security except in the case of a group of men who are likely to have been unemployed and who are most likely to be dissatisfied with their economic situation. On the basis of these results, we could not say that economic insecurity leads to a xenophobic reaction – there was no association with migrants and minorities. However, it does lead to a fear of Russia in the minds of some men.

Security and democracy

When all the elements of security and insecurity in this chapter are put together in a multivariate statistical design, we are faced with the following results: the impact of subjective security upon support for democracy in Central and Eastern Europe is smaller than the influence of the macro-economic dimension of the market economy or the micro-economic dimension of post-Communist households, but bigger than the impact of social structure or European values or identity (see Table 7.10). The phenomenon of security versus insecurity contributes 7 per cent of the variance to explain the dependent variable support for democracy. The most important security-related predictor of being a democratic

Table 7.10 Insecurity and democracy

	1996	*1998*	*Change*
NATO membership a good thing	+0.12	+0.12	0
USA no threat	+0.12	+0.19	+7
Russia a threat	+0.21	+0.12	−9
Neighbouring countries a threat	+0.09	*	*
R^2	0.09	0.07	−2
Significance	0.000	0.000	0.000

Source: New Democracies Barometer 4, 5.

Note
*Not done in this country at this time.

post-Communist citizen is to perceive no threat from the United States of America (beta = 0.19). The second most important security issue with an impact upon democracy is the acceptance of membership of NATO as a good thing (beta = 0.12).

Another important variable, which is linked with support for democracy, is that the Russian Federation poses some threat to a specific Central or Eastern European country. This influence of a scenario of a Russian threat is decreasing from a regression coefficient of 0.21 in 1996 to an association of 0.12 in 1998. In 1996, the feeling of threats by neighbouring countries was linked to being democratic, but this association was no longer significant in 1998. All other threats, which have been described in this chapter, are not significant in relation to support for democracy.

8 European identity, enlargement and support for democracy

European identity and European integration

The first section of this chapter deals with the question of the existence and the extent of a 'European identity' in post-Communist Central and Eastern Europe. Which post-Communist citizens identify with Europe either as a first or as a second identity?

One distinctive feature about European identity in post-Communist Europe is that the number of 'Europeans' in Central and Eastern Europe has been growing during the process of transition. If all eleven countries are taken together, then the mean share of persons with a European identity was 16 per cent in 1991 and *increased* to 22 per cent in 1998 (see Table 8.1). More than every fifth post-Communist citizen in Central and Eastern Europe regards themselves as 'European', which appears to be quite considerable. The highest proportion of people with a European identity

Table 8.1 Europeans in post-Communist Europe

	1991	1996	1998	Diff. 1991–8
Accession countries				
Bulgaria	13	*	24	+11
Slovenia	16	6	21	+5
Slovakia	12	16	20	+8
Czech Republic	15	13	18	+3
Hungary	21	10	*	−11
Poland	15	7	17	+2
Romania	21	13	16	−5
Other countries				
Croatia	*	21	24	+3
FR of Yugoslavia	*	*	23	0
Belarus	*	12	19	+7
Ukraine	*	6	14	+8

Source: New Democracies Barometer 1, 4, 5.

Note
* Not done in this country at this time.
Percentage of people for whom European identity comes first or second.

can be found in Bulgaria, where 24 per cent of all Bulgarians regard themselves as 'Europeans'. The share of 'Europeans' is comparatively very high in the successor states of Yugoslavia: 24 per cent of the Croatian population think of themselves as 'European', 23 per cent of the inhabitants of the Federal Republic of Yugoslavia are 'Europeans' and 21 per cent of Slovenian citizens identify themselves with Europe. It is interesting that in Slovakia the share of Slovaks with a European identity grew from 12 per cent in 1991 to 20 per cent in 1998 despite the specific policy direction of the former Slovak government under Prime Minister Meciar, which was very sceptical, if not negative towards Europe. In Belarus, the group of Byelorussians with a European identity increased from 12 per cent in 1996 to 19 per cent in 1998. In 1991, only 15 per cent of the Czech population regarded themselves as 'Europeans', a figure which went up to 18 per cent in spring 1998. The only country where the subjective identification with Europe went down to a considerable extent was Hungary, where 21 per cent of the Hungarian population regarded themselves as 'Europeans' in 1991. The share of Hungarians with a European identity went down to 10 per cent in 1996. In Poland, the picture is very similar to the Czech Republic. At the beginning of the process of transformations, 15 per cent of the Poles labelled themselves as 'Europeans', a figure which went up to 17 per cent in 1998. In 1991, we find 21 per cent of the Romanians regarded themselves as 'Europeans'. This group decreased to 16 per cent of the Romanian population with a primary or secondary European identity in 1998. As in Belarus, the number of Europeans increased also in another post-Soviet Republic, in the Ukraine: only 6 per cent of the Ukrainian population displayed a European identity in 1996. The share of 'Europeans' in the Ukraine more than doubled between 1996 and 1998 and is now 14 per cent.

If one analyses the impact of gender upon a European identity, the results show that gender matters with regard to the extent of European identity in these ten Central and Eastern European countries. Hungary is not included in this analysis, because the identity question was not asked in the Hungarian survey in 1998. In all ten countries together, we find 24 per cent of men regard themselves as 'Europeans', whereas only 19 per cent of all post-Communist women display a primary or secondary European identity. The gender gap across all nations is 5 per cent between women and men; men in all those countries except Croatia are more oriented towards Europe in terms of their subjective identification than women (see Table 8.2). The gender gap is greatest in Bulgaria: almost one-third of Bulgarian men (29 per cent) display a European identity, whereas only one-fifth of Bulgarian women describe themselves as having a primary or secondary European identity. In the Ukraine, we find a similar pattern of subjective identities: 19 per cent of men, but only 11 per cent of women, claim to have a European identity in the Ukraine. In the Federal Republic of Yugoslavia, 26 per cent of all men identify themselves with Europe and only 20 per cent

Table 8.2 Gender and European identity

	Female	*Male*	*Diff. M–F*	*Mean*
Accession countries				
Bulgaria	20	29	+9	24
Czech Republic	15	21	+6	18
Romania	13	19	+6	16
Slovenia	19	23	+4	21
Slovakia	18	21	+3	20
Poland	17	18	+1	17
Other countries				
Ukraine	11	19	+8	14
FR of Yugoslavia	20	26	+6	23
Belarus	18	20	+2	19
Croatia	25	24	−1	24

Source: New Democracies Barometer 5 (1998).

of all women in Serbia and Montenegro show a subjective European identity. The gender gap is quite considerable in the Czech Republic too: 21 per cent of all Czech men label themselves as Europeans, but only 15 per cent of all Czech women identify with Europe. Well above the average is also the gender gap in Romania: 19 per cent of Romanian men consider themselves as 'European', whereas only 13 per cent of all Romanian women express a primary or secondary identification with Europe.

The gender gap concerning European identity is much smaller in Slovenia and in Slovakia: in Slovenia, we find 23 per cent male 'Europeans' and 19 per cent female 'Europeans', in Slovakia the pattern is very similar. More than one-fifth of Slovak men (21 per cent) show a subjective identification with Europe, whereas only 18 per cent of Slovak women regard themselves as 'Europeans' in terms of territorial identity.

Finally, in Belarus, Poland and Croatia, the size of the gender gap is within the potential sampling error of the survey; we can hypothesise that there is no gender gap in those three countries; sex does not differentiate the identity patterns regarding a European identity in Poland, Croatia and Belarus.

Analysis of the impact of age upon the extent of a European identity in Central and Eastern Europe shows a clear correlation between age and subjective identification in the majority of post-Communist countries analysed: in the whole territory we find 12 per cent of the old generation above 60 years of age describe themselves as 'Europeans'. The share of Europeans goes up in the 'active age group' between 30 and 59 years: 22 per cent of the middle-age group has a primary or secondary form of European identity. The clear-cut core group of 'Europeans' in Central and Eastern Europe is the young generation between 18 and 29 years of age: within this youngest age group, 25 per cent label themselves as 'Europeans'. Therefore one might put forward the hypothesis that the younger the post-Communist citizen, the higher the extent of European identity, an inverse relationship between age and level of subjective identification with Europe (see Table 8.3).

As with the gender gap, the age gap is highest in Bulgaria: 38 per cent of the young Bulgarians under 30 years declare themselves to be Europeans, whereas only 16 per cent of the older generation in Bulgaria identify to some extent with Europe. Exactly the same generation gap is visible in Serbia and Montenegro: only 10 per cent of the Serbs above 60 years show some form of identification with Europe on the one hand, but 32 per cent of the young generation in Serbia and Montenegro describe themselves as Europeans in different degrees of intensity. The generation gap is quite visible in both former Soviet Republics: one-quarter of the Byelorussian youth (26 per cent) expresses a European identity, but only 8 per cent of the older inhabitants of Belarus regard themselves as 'Europeans'. In the Ukraine, the age distribution is very similar to Belarus: 23 per cent of the young Ukrainians under 30 years of age call themselves 'Europeans', whereas only 7 per cent of the Ukrainians above 60 years of age identify with Europe. Age is differentiating Croatian society with regard to European identity too: 17 per cent of the older Croats label themselves as 'Europeans', which is very much in contrast to the Croatian youth, where one-third (33 per cent) display either a primary or a secondary European identity. The generation gap in Slovakia is as high as in Croatia or in the Ukraine: only 12 per cent of the older Slovak generation identifies with Europe, whereas 27 per cent of the Slovak youth regard themselves as 'Europeans'.

Table 8.3 Age and European identity

	Young 18–29	Active 30–59	Old >60	Diff.
Accession countries				
Bulgaria	38	25	16	22
Slovakia	27	18	12	15
Poland	19	18	13	6
Slovenia	18	25	13	12
Czech Republic	18	20	13	7
Romania	17	17	12	5
Other countries				
Croatia	33	22	17	16
FR of Yugoslavia	32	22	10	22
Belarus	26	20	8	18
Ukraine	23	14	7	16

Source: New Democracies Barometer 5 (1998).

Note
Percentage calling themselves European.

In Slovenia, the Czech Republic and Poland, the correlation between young age and higher levels of European identity and the phenomenon of the youth as a core group of 'Europeans' is not as clear-cut as in Bulgaria, Serbia-Montenegro, Croatia, Belarus, the Ukraine and Slovakia. In those three countries within the Central European buffer zone, which are all candidates for the enlargement of the European Union, the differences between the generations are much smaller than in the other countries. In Slovenia, the share of 'Europeans' is at 25 per cent highest in the middle age category between 30 and 59 years, whereas only 18 per cent of the Slovenian youth see themselves as 'Europeans'. In the Czech Republic, 20 per cent of the middle generation between 30 and 59 years show the highest level of European identification. Only 18 per cent of the Czech youth display a primary or secondary European identification. In Poland, the share of Europeans within the Polish youth is at 19 per cent roughly the same as in the middle Polish generation, where 18 per cent declare themselves as 'Europeans'. The distribution is even in Romania between the young generation with 17 per cent 'Europeans' and the middle generation with 17 per cent 'Europeans' too.

Analysis of the impact of education upon the level and extent of European identity in post-Communist Europe shows a very clear pattern, which is visible in all countries: the higher the level of education of a post-Communist citizen, the higher the probability of a European identity. If all ten countries are analysed together as one geographical unit, we find 12 per cent Europeans among persons with primary education, 17 per cent within the group of post-Communist citizens with vocational training, 23 per cent among persons with a secondary level of education and finally on average 34 per cent of all Central and Eastern European citizens with university education are 'Europeans' (see Table 8.4). The country with

Table 8.4 Education and European identity

	Primary	*Vocational*	*Secondary*	*University*	*Diff.*
Accession countries					
Slovenia	10	19	22	41	31
Slovakia	15	14	22	40	26
Bulgaria	10	*	31	39	29
Czech Republic	9	14	22	35	26
Poland	17	14	18	33	19
Romania	11	14	21	19	10
Other countries					
Croatia	20	24	34	52	32
FR of Yugoslavia	11	15	24	36	25
Belarus	9	21	19	34	25
Ukraine	9	17	17	21	12

Source: New Democracies Barometer 5 (1998).

the highest impact of education upon European identity is Croatia: 52 per cent of all Croatian graduates regard themselves as 'Europeans' at a primary or secondary level, whereas only 20 per cent of Croats with primary education report a subjective European identity. The growth of European identity with increasing levels of education is linear in seven countries, only in Poland, the Ukraine and Romania can we not speak of a linear and positive relationship between increasing levels of education and rising European identity. Within the primary level of education in Slovenia we find 10 per cent 'Europeans'; at the tertiary level of Slovenian university graduates we can see 41 per cent who describe themselves as Europeans. In Bulgaria, the bivariate pattern is similar to Slovenia: 10 per cent of the lowest educational strata are 'Europeans', whereas 39 per cent of the Bulgarian graduates identify with Europe as a territorial unit. In Slovakia, 15 per cent of Slovaks with primary education identify with Europe, and 40 per cent of the Slovak graduates are 'Europeans'.

In the Czech Republic, only 9 per cent of persons with primary education describe themselves as 'Europeans', whereas 35 per cent of all Czech graduates identify with Europe. In the Federal Republic of Yugoslavia, the impact of education upon European identity is almost the same as in the Czech Republic: 11 per cent of Serbs with primary education are 'Europeans' and 36 per cent of Serbian graduates choose Europe as the target of identification. In Belarus, the influence of education upon European identification is very similar to other post-Communist countries: 9 per cent of Byelorussians with primary education are 'Europeans' and 34 per cent of the Byelorussian graduates show a European identification.

In Poland, one-third of the Polish graduates describe themselves as 'Europeans', but the other educational strata in Poland do not show the stable and linear pattern which was visible in other Central European countries. In the Ukraine the impact of education upon European identity is very weak; the differences of levels of European identity between educational strata are very small. The same phenomenon occurs in Romania, where the share of 'Europeans' among Romanians with secondary education, 21 per cent, is higher than the share of Europeans among the Romanian graduates, 19 per cent.

The bivariate analysis of the impact of the urban–rural divide upon European identity in post-Communist Europe showed a clear pattern: the higher the number of inhabitants in a given village or town, the higher the probability of a person developing a European identification. If one analyses the whole territory of Central and Eastern Europe as one unit, one finds that the smallest group of Europeans can be found in villages with less than 5,000 inhabitants, where only 15 per cent declare themselves 'Europeans'. In towns with between 6,000 and 20,000 inhabitants, the average number of persons with a European identity is 21 per cent, whereas we find in cities between 21,000 and 100,000 inhabitants a share of 20 per cent who regard themselves as 'Europeans'. The greatest share of Europeans is visible in large cities with more than 100,000 inhabitants. In the Central and Eastern European capitals and regional centres, on average 27 per cent of the city dwellers have a European identity. Hence, we can argue that the extent of European identity is associated with the degree of urbanisation in post-Communist Europe (see Table 8.5).

The urban–rural divide is very significant in Slovenia, where we find only 14 per cent of 'Europeans' in small villages, but 43 per cent of Slovenians in cities with more than 100,000 inhabitants like Ljubljana identify with Europe. The distribution along the urban–rural dimension in Slovakia is very similar to Slovenia: 12 per cent of Slovakian villagers describe themselves as 'Europeans', whereas 40 per cent of Slovaks, who live in cities like Bratislava or Kosice, identify with Europe as compared to Slovakia, their own region or their town. In the Ukraine, the level of European identity is growing with the size of the community: 9 per cent in Ukrainian villages are 'Europeans', but 17 per cent in cities like Kiev or L'viv show a European identity. The deviant cases within the Ukraine are cities with between 6,000 and 20,000 inhabitants, where we find the greatest share of 'Europeans' with 20 per cent. In Poland, the pattern is again very clear and close to the general pattern of European identity in Central and Eastern Europe: in the Polish villages, 14 per cent of the rural population identify with Europe, whereas in Polish big cities like Warsaw or Krakow 22 per cent of the urban population label themselves as 'Europeans'. The general pattern is also visible in Bulgaria, albeit somewhat smoother and less explicit: in the Bulgarian villages, we do find 20 per cent of the rural population with a 'European identity'. Large Bulgarian cities like Sofia or Plovdiv have almost one-third (29 per cent), who show an emotional affiliation with Europe. In Serbia and Montenegro, the standard pattern of the impact of the urban–rural divide cannot

Table 8.5 Urban–rural divide and European identity

	<5,000	*<20,000*	*<100,000*	*>100,000*	*Diff.*
Accession countries					
Slovenia	14	18	21	43	29
Slovakia	12	20	22	40	28
Bulgaria	20	26	24	29	7
Poland	14	*	16	22	8
Romania	17	11	16	16	6
Other countries					
Croatia	22	26	27	27	5
Belarus	11	20	15	27	16
FR of Yugoslavia	20	27	25	23	7
Ukraine	9	20	14	17	11

Source: New Democracies Barometer 5 (1998).

Note
Percentage who identify with Europe.

be identified. Hence, we cannot speak of a clear and directed association between urbanisation and European identity in the Federal Republic of Yugoslavia. Not only in Serbia and Montenegro, but also in Romania and Croatia, no impact of the urban–rural divide upon European identity could be found. In those two ex-Yugoslav countries and in Romania, the distribution of 'Europeans' is not linked to the size of the place in which they live.

Our next research question is the relationship between having a European identity, on the one hand, and supporting the EU accession of your own country, on the other. Analysis showed that there is a strong association between feeling a European and wishing to join the European Union. The absolute majority of all post-Communist citizens with a European identity (56 per cent) are strongly for their own country joining the European Union (see Table 8.6). A further 36 per cent of all 'Europeans' in Central and Eastern Europe are somewhat for their own country joining the European Union. Together, 92 per cent of all persons with a European identity support the EU accession of the state they are living in. Only a very small minority of 8 per cent of post-Communist Europeans are strongly against joining the European Union. Their concept of 'Europe' is obviously very different from the concept of Europe as represented by the European Union.

The strongest association between Europeans and supporters of EU integration was found in the Federal Republic of Yugoslavia, where 70 per cent of the Serbs with a European identity also strongly support the EU accession of Serbia and Montenegro. Also quite high is the link between European identity and favouring the enlargement of the European Union in Slovakia: 69 per cent of the 'Europeans' in Slovakia very strongly want their country to join the EU. In Croatia, we find a very similar pattern as

Table 8.6 European identity and support for EU accession

	Strongly for	*Somewhat for*	*Against*
Accession countries			
Slovakia	69	25	6
Romania	57	34	10
Slovenia	50	39	11
Czech Republic	48	42	10
Poland	45	47	8
Other countries			
FR of Yugoslavia	70	27	4
Croatia	64	33	3
Belarus	48	43	9

Source: New Democracies Barometer 5 (1998).

Note
Percentage persons with European identity, who are Strongly for/Somewhat for/Against joining the European Union.

in Serbia or in Slovakia: 64 per cent of all Croats with a European identity are strongly for Croatia joining the European Union. The 'Europeans' in Romania link their emotional ties with Europe to a strong support for Romania joining the European Union. The majority of 'Europeans' (57 per cent) very much want the integration of Romania into the European Union.

In Slovenia, the Czech Republic and Poland, the citizens with a European identity also favour the EU accession of their own country, but are less enthusiastic than other countries, which are not candidates for the enlargement of the European Union in the first round. In Slovenia, 50 per cent of the 'Europeans' are strongly and 39 per cent of the 'Europeans' somewhat in favour of Slovenia joining the European Union. The same pattern could be found in the Czech Republic, where 48 per cent of the 'Europeans' are strongly and 42 per cent of the 'Europeans' are somewhat in favour of the Czech Republic joining the EU. In Poland, the 'Europeans' are even more for a wait-and-see strategy: 45 per cent of the Polish population who identify with Europe are strongly in favour of the Polish EU accession, whereas a further 47 per cent of the Polish 'Europeans' are only somewhat in favour of the integration of Poland within the European Union. In Belarus, the interesting fact is that having a European identity in Belarus also means that the same person favours the EU membership of Belarus.

The enlargement of the European Union: a view from the East

How polarised or homogeneous are the general public with regard to the prospect of their own country joining the European Union in the foreseeable future? One basic question related to the enlargement of the European Union towards Central Europe, on the one hand, and South and Eastern Europe, on the other, is the image which is associated with the political institution of the European Union in the former Communist parts of Europe. The general image of the European Union improved quite considerably between 1994, when it was first measured by the New Democracies Barometer and by the Russian Federation Survey, and 1998 (see Table 8.7). When all eleven post-Communist countries are taken together, an average of 37 per cent had positive impressions of the aims and activities of the European Union in 1994, a value which increased to 63 per cent of all post-Communist citizens four years later, in 1998. The biggest improvement of the EU image could be found in the candidate states of Central Europe: in Central Europe the share of persons with a positive image of the European Union doubled from 32 per cent in 1994 to 66 per cent in 1998! One might argue that the image of the EU in the Central European buffer zone passed through a phase of dramatic improvement in those four years between 1994 and 1998. In Southern and

Table 8.7 European Union image in post-Communist Europe

Q. As you might know, fifteen states of Western Europe together form the European Union. Would you say that your impressions of the aims and activities of the European Community are generally positive, neutral or negative?

	1994	*1998*	*Diff.*
Accession countries			
Slovenia	35	71	+36
Czech Republic	34	68	+34
Poland	34	65	+31
Slovakia	27	64	+37
Hungary	28	62	+34
Romania	57	61	+4
Bulgaria	42	58	+16
Other countries			
Croatia	20	76	+56
FR of Yugoslavia	*	58	0
Belarus	47	49	+2
Ukraine	51	44	−7
Russia	25	*	0

Sources: New Democracies Barometer 3; 1994; N = 14.622. New Democracies Barometer 5; 1998; N = 11.296.

Note
*Not done in this country at this time.
Percentage who are positive.

Eastern Europe, the image of the European Union was better than in Central Europe in 1994 with 43 per cent having a positive impression of the aims and activities of the European Union. The experience of not being included in the first round of candidates for EU enlargement obviously cooled down the enthusiastic impressions of the European Union in these countries: in 1998, only 58 per cent had a positive impression of the EU, which was an increase since 1994, but is well below the EU image in Central Europe.

Among the candidates for the first round of enlargement of the European Union, the image of the EU is consistently the best in Slovenia: in 1994, 35 per cent of the Slovenian population had a positive impression of the aims and activities of the EU, which was the best image in Central Europe. In 1998, the absolute majority of 71 per cent of all Slovenes had a positive image of the European Union. The EU image is very high in a consistent manner in the Czech Republic: 34 per cent of the Czech population had positive impressions of the EU in 1994, which doubled to 68 per cent of all Czech citizens in 1998, who described a positive image of the European Union. The third best image of the European Union we find in a constant way over time in Poland. As in the Czech Republic, in Slovakia and in Hungary, the group with a positive EU image in Poland doubled in the course of the past years from 34 per cent in 1994 to 65 per cent in 1998. The image of the European Union in Slovakia has the same distribution as in the other Central European countries which are candidates for the first round of EU enlargement. In 1994, only 27 per cent of the Slovak population had positive impressions of the activities of the European Union, whereas we see a steep increase to 64 per cent of the Slovak general public who showed a positive image of the EU in spring 1998 during the last stage of the Meciar era, ending in autumn 1998. The image of the EU in Hungary is at the same level as in Poland and Slovakia: in 1994, only 28 per cent of the Hungarian population were positively impressed by the European Union. That low profile of the EU image in Hungarian society improved significantly in the following four years: in 1998, already 62 per cent of Hungarians showed positive impressions of the aims and activities of the European Union in the late 1990s.

In Croatia, the perception of the European Union was blurred by the war on the territory of former Yugoslavia and the European Union as actor in the international attempts to end that terrible European war. The involvement of the EU, which was partly expressed by putting the Croatian government under political and military pressure, had the effect that only 20 per cent of the Croatian population had a positive image of the European Union in 1994, when the war was still going on. In the period after the Dayton Agreement, the interactions between Croatia and the EU started to normalise and the Croatian population developed a very good image of the European Union: in 1998, a record 76 per cent of all Croats had positive impressions of the aims and behaviour of the European Union, which is by far the highest share compared to all the other ten post-Communist societies. In Romania, the EU image was extremely good in 1994, when 57 per cent of Romanian society expressed a positive EU image. Due to the short-term exclusion of Romania for enlargement, that share went only slightly up to 61 per cent in 1998, showing the disappointment of the Romanian general public about the decision of the European Union not to include Romania in the first round of enlargement. In Bulgaria, the EU image was quite good in 1994 and improved to 58 per cent of the Bulgarians who had positive impressions of the European Union, in 1998. The disappointment of being excluded from the first round of EU enlargement was not as strong in Bulgaria as in Romania, maybe because the Bulgarian population were not very hopeful concerning the EU accession of their own country anyway. A very interesting phenomenon can be observed in Serbia and Montenegro. Despite the fact that the European Union has been constantly exerting political and – in joint operations with NATO – military pressure upon the Federal Republic of Yugoslavia during the past years, the Serbian public expresses with a high percentage of 58 per cent that their impressions of the aims and activities of the European Union, which causes a lot of trouble for the Serbian government, are positive! Hence, the image of the European Union in Serbia and Montenegro is not as bad as one might think after the international events on the territory of former Yugoslavia and during the current crisis in Kosovo. This gives some hope for the future concerning the attitude of the Serbian population towards European integration and the role of the European Union in that important transnational process. In Belarus and in the Ukraine, the pattern over time regarding the image of the European Union in those former Soviet Republics is very similar: in 1994, the absolute majority of the Ukrainians and 47 per cent of the Byelorussia population had a positive image of the European Union. In the Russian Federation, one-quarter of the Russians (25 per cent) had positive impressions of the aims and activities of the European Union, which is considerably less than in Belarus and the Ukraine and shows a somewhat greater distance of the Russian citizens towards the European Union. Nevertheless, in Russia the image of the EU in 1994 was similar to the level in Slovakia, where only 27 per cent had a positive image of the EU, a phenomenon which has changed considerably since.

Together with Romania, we found the best EU image in the Ukraine and in Belarus, if compared between all eleven post-Communist countries in 1994. The experience in Belarus and the Ukraine between 1994 and 1998 that the enlargement process will not reach Kiev and Minsk has cooled down all expectations of Ukrainians and Byelorussians about any closer links with the EU in the foreseeable future, let alone EU accession. Hence, the percentage of the Ukrainian population with a positive EU image went down from 51 per cent in 1994 to 44 per cent in 1998. The EU image in Belarus stayed rather stable with 49 per cent of the Byelorussian general public in 1998, which show a positive image of the EU. The image of the European Union in the Russian Federation is quite different to the attitudinal patterns in Belarus and the Ukraine: 33 per cent of all Russians are neutral concerning the EU, 40 per cent have either no opinion or do not know what the EU is about, and finally 25 per cent of the Russian population have positive impressions of the aims and the activities of the European Union.

How deeply embedded is the wish of the ordinary Czech or Pole to join the EU? The first impression is that the overwhelming majority of the Central European, Southern European and Eastern European general public express the wish to join the European Union; the citizens of all eleven countries want their home country to be integrated into the European Union in the process of EU enlargement to the East in the years to come (see Table 8.8). The mean value for all eleven countries of the share of post-Communist citizens who are strongly in favour of their own country joining the European Union is more than one-third over time: in 1994, 37 per cent of all post-Communist citizens were strongly in favour of EU accession; this figure remained at 36 per cent in 1996, roughly the same in the course of those four years, if one looks at all eleven New Democracies without any regional distinction.

If the post-Communist universe is split into the Central European part, on the one hand, and the South-Eastern European part, on the other, we

Table 8.8 Attitudes towards EU enlargement

	Strongly 1994	Somewhat	Total	Strongly 1998	Somewhat	Total
Accession countries						
Romania	59	36	95	37	51	88
Poland	26	59	85	33	54	87
Hungary	35	52	87	33	52	85
Slovakia	34	55	89	40	44	84
Slovenia	24	72	96	31	51	82
Czech Republic	33	56	89	33	47	80
Bulgaria	51	37	88	*	*	*
Other countries						
Ukraine	43	53	96	*	*	*
Croatia	34	60	94	54	41	95
Belarus	32	53	85	27	55	82
FR of Yugoslavia	*	*	*	37	45	82
Russia	26	39	65	*	*	*

Sources: New Democracies Barometer 3; 1994; N = 14.622. New Democracies Barometer 5; 1998; N = 11.296.

Note
* Not done in this country at this time.
Percentage in favour.

see divergent patterns of longitudinal development with regard to general public attitudes towards the enlargement of the European Union. The core group of strong supporters of EU accession within the Central European buffer zone grew from 30 per cent in 1994 to 34 per cent in 1998, whereas the core group of Eastern Europeans, who are strongly in favour of their own country joining the European Union, shrank from 44 per cent in 1994 to 39 per cent in 1998. Hence, we can hypothesise that the Central European citizens are moving faster towards European integration than the Eastern European citizens, who are feeling the slowdown of the process of European integration as far as their own country is concerned and are reacting with a reduction of strong support for EU membership. Nevertheless, the overwhelming majority of 85 per cent of all post-Communist citizens are strongly or somewhat in favour of their own country joining the European Union, which shows in a very clear manner that the European Union is seen as *the* option for European transnational integration for the post-Communist citizenry.

The support for EU accession within the Central European buffer zone is highest in Poland after a pro-EU shift during the period between 1994 and 1998 in Polish society. In 1994, only 26 per cent of the Polish population were strong supporters of Poland joining the EU, whereas that share went up to 33 per cent of all Poles in 1998. Altogether, 87 per cent of the Polish general public support the integration of Poland into the

European Union, which is the record value in comparison with all other post-Communist countries during the period observed. Support for EU accession is also high in Hungary, where 35 per cent of the Hungarian population in 1994 and 33 per cent of all Hungarians strongly support the integration of Hungary into the European Union. The support for Hungary joining the EU was very high and stable between 1994 and 1998. The pattern in Slovakia concerning the question of EU membership is very similar, if compared with the other candidates for the first round of EU accession. In 1994, 34 per cent of all Slovaks were strongly in favour of their homeland joining the European Union. This core group of support of EU accession in Slovakia grew to 40 per cent of the Slovakian general public in 1998, which makes Slovakia prepared for EU integration, at least at the level of general public support. In Slovenia the support for EU membership was extremely high in 1994, when 96 per cent of all Slovenes supported the EU accession of Slovenia. That record level of EU support in Slovenia decreased to a 'normal' level of 82 per cent in 1998 and we can justly talk of a process of normalisation concerning the attitudinal patterns in Slovenia regarding EU membership. In the Czech Republic, the general public attitudes towards EU integration were frozen between 1994 and 1998: in both years, 33 per cent of the Czech population strongly supported the integration of the Czech Republic into the European Union. The total number of Czech supporters for EU accession went down from 89 per cent in 1994 to 80 per cent in 1998. The general level of EU support within Czech society reflects the political and economic 'depression' of the Czech electorate, which could be found at the end of the 'Klaus era' in spring 1998 (Wallace and Haerpfer 1998).

Support for the EU was the highest in 1994 in the Ukraine with a total support of 96 per cent, but we do not have figures for 1998, unfortunately. In the Ukraine in 1994, a majority of 43 per cent strongly supported the integration of their homeland into the European Union, the EU being one of the few hopes for economic recovery and political stability in that crisis-stricken large country. The highest level of long-term support for EU accession in Southern and Eastern Europe was identified in Croatia. The share of strong supporters of Croatia joining the European Union went up from 34 per cent in 1994 to an absolute majority of 54 per cent of all Croats in 1998, which is the highest value for all post-Communist countries which have been analysed. A total of 95 per cent of the Croatian general public is strongly or somewhat supportive of the integration of Croatia into the European Union, which is also a record level compared to all other states. The Romanian euphoria about EU membership in 1994, when 59 per cent of all Romanians were strongly supportive of EU accession, was replaced by realism about the long-term chances of Romania joining the EU in 1998, when only 37 per cent of the Romanian population formed the core group of support for Romanian integration as part of European enlargement. In Bulgaria, the wish to join the European

Union was strongly supported by an absolute majority of 51 per cent of the Bulgarian general public in 1994. In Belarus, the strong support for EU membership decreased from 32 per cent in 1994 to 27 per cent in 1998, indicating also a more distant perspective of the Byelorussian electorate about the political chances of Belarus becoming part of the European Union in the foreseeable future. Despite the strong international impact of the European Union during the wars on the territory of former Yugoslavia, 82 per cent of the population in Serbia and Montenegro supported the idea of the Federal Republic of Yugoslavia joining the European Union in 1998. In the Russian Federation finally, 65 per cent of the Russian Federation supported the membership of Russia in the European Union, which appears to be quite surprising. There is a core group of 26 per cent of the Russian population between Moscow and the far east of the Russian Federation who even strongly supported the concept of an EU enlargement including Russia in 1994, when our large Russian survey was conducted.

There is a clear-cut impact of gender upon the attitudes of post-Communist citizens towards transnational integration into the European Union. Male respondents are much more in favour of EU accession than women (see Table 8.9). If all Central and Eastern Europeans are taken together, 40 per cent of all men but only 33 per cent of all women are strongly in favour of their own country joining the European Union. In the Central European buffer zone, 38 per cent of Central European men and only 31 per cent of women in that group of candidates for the first round of enlargement were strongly in favour of EU accession. In South-East Europe the distribution is similar, albeit at a higher level: 43 per cent of men in Eastern and Southern Europe, but only 37 per cent of women

Table 8.9 Gender and EU accession

Q. If your country were to join the European Union in the future, would you feel strongly in favour?

	Percentage women	*Percentage men*	*Diff.*
Accession countries			
Poland	31	35	+4
Czech Republic	31	35	+4
Romania	35	39	+4
Slovenia	27	35	+8
Hungary	29	39	+10
Slovakia	35	45	+10
Other countries			
Croatia	55	54	−1
Russia	23	30	+7
FR of Yugoslavia	36	46	+10
Belarus	22	33	+11

Sources: New Democracies Barometer 5 (1998). Russian Federation Survey 1994; N = 3.535.

in that European region are for joining the European Union. There seems to be a gender gap of approximately 7 per cent between the sexes, with male post-Communist citizens being much more supportive of transnational integration into the European Union.

In the Central European buffer zone, the gender gap is biggest in Slovakia and Hungary. The Slovakian men strongly support the integration of Slovakia in the EU with a share of 45 per cent, whereas only 35 per cent of Slovakian women are in the core group for EU enlargement. In a similar way, 39 per cent of male Hungarians form the core group of support for Hungary joining the European Union. The concept of Hungary as a future full member of the European union is favoured by a much smaller group of 29 per cent of female Hungarians. In Slovenia, we find 35 per cent of men and a smaller group of 27 per cent of women who are strongly in favour of Slovenia joining the European Union in the first round of enlargement. Within Central Europe, the gender gap is smallest in Poland and the Czech Republic with male dominance of 4 per cent. In the Czech Republic, 35 per cent of Czech men and 31 per cent of Czech women constitute the avant-garde for bringing the Czech Republic into the European Union. In Poland, the distribution by gender is exactly the same as in the Czech Republic, with 35 per cent of male Poles and 31 per cent of female Poles representing that important third of the Polish electorate, which is strongly in favour of Poland as a future member state of the EU.

In South-East Europe, the impact of gender upon EU accession is quite similar to the observed pattern in Central Europe. In all countries except Croatia we find male dominance concerning the individual support for EU accession, as is the case in Central Europe.

In Belarus, 33 per cent of the male population and 22 per cent of the female population can be regarded as the core group of people supporting the integration of Belarus into the European Union. In the Federal Republic of Yugoslavia, 46 per cent of men and 36 per cent of women want Serbia and Montenegro soon to join the European Union. The gender gap is comparatively low in Romania with a distance of 4 per cent between men and women: 39 per cent of male Romanians are for Romanian EU accession compared to 35 per cent of female Romanians. Croatia finally is the deviant case in that analysis of the influence of gender upon attitudes towards EU accession. In Croatia, we find slightly more women than men in the core group of strong support for EU accession: 55 per cent of all Croatian women and 54 per cent of all Croatian men are strongly in favour of Croatia becoming a member of the European Union.

Analysis of the impact of age upon EU accession in post-Communist Europe showed a clear and promising overall picture: the core group of support for the enlargement of the European Union to the East is primarily the post-Communist youth. The younger the respondent, the higher the support for joining the European Union (see Table 8.10). The age cohort with the highest levels of sympathy for joining the EU are the

Table 8.10 Age and EU accession

Q. If our country were to join the European Union in the future, would you feel strongly in favour?

	18–29 years	*30–59 years*	*>60 years*	*Diff.*
Accession countries				
Romania	50	35	24	+26
Slovakia	43	42	27	+16
Slovenia	39	30	24	+15
Poland	38	30	27	+11
Hungary	37	35	27	+10
Czech Republic	36	33	30	+6
Other countries				
Croatia	57	54	51	+6
FR of Yugoslavia	52	41	20	+32
Russia	35	26	16	+19
Belarus	34	26	21	+13

Sources: New Democracies Barometer 5 (1998); N = 11.296. Russian Federation Survey (1994); N = 3.535.

young people in all countries together between 18 and 29 years: within that age group of post-Communist youth, 43 per cent 'feel strongly in favour' of EU accession.

Around the overall NDB mean is the support for EU accession in the middle age group between 30 and 59 years: 36 per cent of this active part of the population are 'strongly in favour' of joining the European Union. In the age group above 60 years, only 28 per cent 'feel strongly in favour' of their home country joining the EU. The difference between generations with regard to EU accession is bigger in South-East Europe than in Central Europe. In South-East Europe, 48 per cent of the people younger than 30 years of age strongly support the integration of their own country into the European Union. Obviously, they put a lot of hope in such a process of transnational integration for their own future. The middle part of the population in South-East Europe supports, with a share of 39 per cent, the enlargement process of the EU. Within the older generation in Southern and Eastern Europe, we find 29 per cent who strongly support the EU accession of their own country. In Central Europe, 39 per cent of the young Central Europeans form the core group in favour of integrating the candidate countries for the first round of enlargement. One-third (34 per cent) of the middle age group and 27 per cent of the older generation in Central Europe are very much in favour of EU accession of the Czech Republic, Hungary, Poland, Slovakia and Slovenia respectively.

In the Central European buffer zone, the age differences with regard to EU accession are biggest in Slovakia and Slovenia. In Slovakia, 43 per cent of young Slovaks under 30 years of age can be seen as strong supporters of the integration of Slovakia into the European Union, whereas only 27 per cent of the older Slovaks above 60 years of age have a strong sympathy for EU accession. A very similar pattern, compared with Slovakia, was found in Slovenia. The Slovenian youth forms, with a share of 39 per cent, the core group of strong support for the integration of Slovenia into the European Union. That strong support goes down to 30 per cent in the middle age group between 30 and 59 years and finally only one-quarter (24 per cent) of the older Slovenian generation strongly supports the integration of Slovenia within the European Union. The age gap concerning EU accession is very similar in Poland and Hungary with a difference of approximately 10 per cent between the youth and the elderly and a clear-cut dominance of young people in the process of integration. The integration of Hungary is strongly supported by 37 per cent of Hungarian youth; Polish EU membership is decisively backed by 38 per cent of the young Poles. One-third of the middle generation strongly supports EU accession in Poland and Hungary, whereas exactly 27 per cent of the older Poles and older Hungarians are in favour of joining the European Union. The influence of age upon EU accession is somehow smaller in the Czech Republic with an age gap of only 6 per cent. Only 36 per cent of the Czech youth are very much in favour of EU accession, followed by 33 per cent of the Czech middle generation and 30 per cent of the older Czechs.

The distribution of age groups is more heterogeneous in South-East Europe than in Central Europe; the age gap is much bigger in the former countries. The biggest age differences we find in the Federal Republic of Yugoslavia with a cleavage of 32 per cent between the young and the elderly with respect to EU integration. The absolute majority of 52 per cent of young people from Serbia and Montenegro are very much in favour of EU accession of their own country, which shows the enormous hopes associated with such a process of integration of a country, which is very much isolated internationally in the course of the 1990s. On the other side of the polarised Serbian society, only 20 per cent of the older generation above 60 years of age strongly support EU accession of the Federal Republic of Yugoslavia. The age divide is also quite wide in Romania with a distance of 26 per cent between the Romanian youth and the older generation. The absolute majority of 50 per cent of young Romanians under 30 years of age strongly supports Romania joining the European Union, whereas only 24 per cent of the older Romanians above 60 years of age are in favour of EU accession. On the territory of the former Soviet Union, the age divide is not as big as in Serbia or Romania. In the Russian Federation the age gap amounts to 19 per cent with a share of 35 per cent of young Russians who are strongly in favour of Russia becoming a member of the European Union. It appears to be quite an astonishing phenomenon that more than one-third of the Russian youth is very much in favour of EU accession of the Russian Federation. One-quarter of the Russian middle generation (26 per cent) is strongly in favour of EU membership of the Russian Federation, whereas only 16 per cent of the older Russians above 60 years display a strong preference for the EU accession of Russia. The age distribution in Belarus is almost exactly the same as in the Russian Federation: one-third of the young people in Belarus (34 per cent) are very much in favour of Belarus becoming a EU member state, one-quarter (26 per cent) of the middle generation favours EU accession and one-fifth (21 per cent) of the old generation in Belarus like the idea of their country being integrated within the European Union.

We found a clear pattern concerning the impact of education upon attitudes towards EU accession in Central Europe, on the one hand, and in South-East Europe, on the other: rising levels of education result in higher support for accession to the European Union (see Table 8.11). If all the countries are analysed together, the following pattern concerning the influence of education upon EU accession arises. The primary level of education consists only of 28 per cent who 'feel strongly in favour' of joining the EU. The vocational level of education displays a higher level of support: 34 per cent of people with vocational education strongly approve of EU membership. Approximately one-third (31 per cent) of respondents with secondary education are strongly in favour of EU integration. The highest level of support for EU membership can be found in the group with tertiary education: within the group of post-Communist citizens with university degrees 50 per cent support in a clear-cut and strong way the EU membership of their home country.

In the Central European buffer zone, one-quarter of people with primary education (26 per cent) are strongly in favour of joining the European Union; this share goes up to approximately one-third (31 per cent) of all Central Europeans with vocational education. At the

Table 8.11 Education and EU accession

	Primary education	Secondary education	Vocational education	University education	Diff.
Accession countries					
Slovakia	28	35	46	68	+40
Czech Republic	22	30	37	51	+29
Hungary	22	33	41	47	+25
Slovenia	28	27	31	46	+19
Romania	24	37	43	43	+19
Poland	32	29	36	36	+7
Other countries					
Croatia	52	56	57	66	+14
FR of Yugoslavia	23	33	44	56	+33
Russia	16	28	24	36	+20
Belarus	17	29	31	35	+18

Sources: New Democracies Barometer 5 (1998). Russian Federation Survey 1994; N = 3.535.

Note
Percentage strongly in favour of EU accession.

secondary level of education in Central Europe, we find 38 per cent who are very much in favour of EU membership of their country. Every second Central European graduate with a first or second university degree (50 per cent) strongly supports the EU membership of the candidates for the first round of EU enlargement. Hence, we can hypothesise that the tertiary level of education is the core group of support for EU accession within the Central European buffer zone and that we see a clear and linear pattern of association between levels of education and support for enlargement of the European Union in that region alongside the current 'Schengen border' of the EU.

With regard to the educational divide in post-Communist societies, we find very similar attitudinal patterns in the Czech Republic and Slovakia, which had been previously parts of one state – Czechoslovakia – until December 1991 and split in January 1992. The educational gap is by far the highest in Slovakia with a 40 per cent difference between the primary level and the tertiary level of education. Slovaks with primary education support the EU integration of Slovakia with a share of 28 per cent, Slovaks with secondary education are in favour of EU accession with 46 per cent, whereas the absolute majority of 68 per cent of university graduates are very much in favour of Slovakia becoming a member state of the EU, which is the highest proportion of EU supporters by educational strata, if compared with all other post-Communist states. In the Czech Republic one-fifth of Czechs with primary education (22 per cent) support EU accession, more than one-third (37 per cent) of Czech citizens with secondary education and every second Czech university graduate (51 per cent) are strongly in favour of the Czech Republic becoming a member of the European Union in the medium-term perspective. In Hungary, one-fifth of Hungarians with primary education (22 per cent), 41 per cent of Hungarian citizens with secondary education and 47 per cent of Hungarian graduates are strongly in favour of Hungary joining the European Union during the first round of EU enlargement. Slovakia, the Czech Republic and Hungary show a clear correlation between levels of education and increasing support for EU accession. In Slovenia and Poland, this general trend, which is visible in Central Europe and in South-East Europe, does not exist in such a linear way. In Slovenia, the dividing line is drawn between university graduates, on the one hand, and all other educational strata, on the other. Roughly one-third of the primary level of education (28 per cent) of Slovenes with vocational education (27 per cent) and of Slovenian citizens with secondary education (31 per cent) strongly support EU accession of Slovenia, displaying more or less the same size of this core group of EU support. On the other side of the educational divide, 46 per cent of all Slovenian university graduates support strongly the future EU membership of Slovenia. In Poland, we do not find any pattern concerning the influence of education upon EU accession; Polish society is quite homogeneous with regard to Polish membership in the EU, if one looks at different educational strata.

In every educational strata of Polish society, we see more or less one-third, who are strongly in favour of Poland joining the EU in the course of the first round of enlargement.

Within Southern and Eastern Europe, the impact of education upon EU accession is clearly visible with educational gaps between 14 and 33 per cent differentiating rising levels of education. Serbian society is again very heterogeneous in terms of different educational strata: one-quarter of Serbs with primary education (23 per cent) and 44 per cent of persons with secondary education are in favour of Serbia-Montenegro joining the European Union. The highest level of support for the EU accession of Serbia-Montenegro can be found at the tertiary level of education: the absolute majority of 56 per cent of all Serbian university graduates strongly support the integration of the Federal Republic of Yugoslavia into the European Union in the future.

In Romania, the educational divide consists of persons with primary education and vocational education, on the one hand, and people with secondary and tertiary education on the other. One-quarter of Romanians with primary education (24 per cent) are strongly in favour of the EU accession of Romania and more than one-third of persons with vocational education (37 per cent) are among the core group backing EU enlargement in Romania. The secondary and tertiary level education in Romania display exactly the same extent of support for EU accession: in both educational strata, 43 per cent each declare that they are very much in favour of Romania becoming a member state of the European Union. Belarus follows the standard pattern visible in post-Communist Europe: 17 per cent of Byelorussians with primary education, 31 per cent of persons with secondary education and 35 per cent of university graduates in Belarus can be labelled as the core group supporting the future EU membership of this post-Soviet state. In Croatia, the influence of education upon EU accession is visible, but not as strongly as in other South-East European countries: 52 per cent of Croats with primary education are strongly in favour of Croatia joining the European Union, 57 per cent of the secondary level of education and finally 66 per cent of all Croatian university graduates can be described as the core group of support for the EU accession of Croatia.

Another interesting research question posed by this book was whether the income of the individual household had any impact upon the attitudes towards EU accession. The main result was that higher levels of income correlated positively with higher levels of support for EU membership (see Table 8.12). First, we looked at all post-Communist countries together in order to identify a possible general pattern across nations. Within the lowest income quartile, only 30 per cent are strongly in favour of EU accession. That share goes up to 34 per cent in the second income quartile and rises further to 39 per cent in the third income quartile in post-Communist Europe. The strongest support for EU membership was found within the highest income quartile, the households with the best

Table 8.12 Household income and EU accession

	Lowest quartile	Second quartile	Third quartile	Highest quartile	Diff.
Accession countries					
Slovakia	27	36	37	57	+30
Romania	23	36	38	48	+25
Slovenia	27	24	34	44	+17
Poland	31	24	35	35	+11
Other countries					
Croatia	46	47	60	63	+17
FR of Yugoslavia	32	40	44	53	+21
Russia	20	21	28	31	+11
Belarus	22	28	26	31	+9

Sources: New Democracies Barometer 5 (= NDB 5) 1998; Russian Federation Survey, 1994; N = 3.535.

Note
income = income of the whole household.
Percentage strongly for joining the EU.

income situation, where 47 per cent are very positive about their country joining the European Union. One might postulate the hypothesis that the winners of micro-economic transformation are the core group of support for the enlargement of the European Union eastwards.

The association between household income and support for EU enlargement exists in Central Europe: 28 per cent of the lowest and second quartiles each are strongly in favour of EU accession, that share goes up to 35 per cent in the third quartile and finally to 45 per cent of the households with the highest incomes. The influence of household income upon EU accession is somewhat clearer in South-East Europe. One-third of the lowest income group (31 per cent) are in favour of EU membership of their own country; this value increases to 38 per cent in the second quartile and 42 per cent in the third quartile. The richest households in Southern and Eastern Europe show the highest level of support (49 per cent) for future membership within an enlarged European Union.

The attitudinal patterns of the impact of the financial situation of an individual household upon the support for enlargement within Central Europe are not very consistent. Only in Slovakia is the hypothesis of a linear association between higher incomes and higher levels of support for EU accession verified. Among the lowest income quartile in the Slovakian income distribution, 27 per cent of the poorest households strongly support EU integration of Slovakia. This share of supporting households goes up to 36 per cent in the second income quartile and further increases in the third income quartile. The highest level of support for Slovakia joining the European Union occurs finally in the highest income group, where the absolute majority of 57 per cent strongly favours the intention of making Slovakia a full member of the European Union. In Slovenia, the pattern is deviant, because the second quartile (24 per cent) shows lower support for EU accession than the poorest Slovenian households (27 per cent). Within the group of the richest Slovenian households, 44 per cent favour the integration of Slovenia into the European Union. In Poland, we do not find a clear influence of household income upon EU accession. The financial situation of Polish households does not appear to matter with regard to the attitudes towards membership of Poland in the European Union.

In South-East Europe, the linear association between the increasing income of households, on the one hand, and stronger support for EU accession, on the other, exists in a much clearer way than in Central Europe. In Romania, the poorest households support the eventual future EU membership of Romania with 23 per cent, whereas 48 per cent of the richest household favour in a decisive way a European enlargement process involving Romania. The income gap is also quite high in the Federal Republic of Yugoslavia: one-third of the poorest Serbian households (32 per cent) favour EU accession; that share goes up constantly with each higher income quartile in Serbia and Montenegro. The highest support for Serbia to join the EU is visible in the highest income group, where the absolute majority of 53 per cent strongly support the entry of the Federal Republic of Yugoslavia into the European Union. The pattern in Croatia is very similar to the pattern in Serbia and Montenegro, albeit at a higher level: 46 per cent of the Croatian households with the lowest income support EU membership of Croatia, this share grows to 60 per cent in the third quartile and culminates in the group of the richest Croatian households, where 63 per cent strongly favour the economic integration of Croatia into the European Union. In Belarus we do not find a clear pattern concerning the impact of household income upon EU accession.

The analysis of attitudes towards the European Union by work and professions shows a clear picture: the new entrepreneurs in the new market economies in Central Europe are the core supporters of integration of national economies into the common market of the European Union (see Table 8.13). The owners of small and medium-sized enterprises (SMEs) are the top occupational group supporting EU enlargement: 48 per cent of small and medium entrepreneurs support the EU accession of their home country. The absolute majority of 46 per cent of owners of large enterprises are 'strongly in favour' of joining the European Union in the future, too. Furthermore, 42 per cent of all self-employed persons 'feel strongly in favour' of EU accession. The new middle class of entrepreneurs and other self-employed persons forms without any doubt the core group of support for an enlargement of the European Union towards post-Communist Europe (Wallace and Haerpfer 1998). The new entrepreneurs obviously hope that joining the European Union will improve their economic position.

Table 8.13 Employment status and EU accession

Q. If our country were to join the European Union in the future, would you feel strongly in favour, somewhat in favour, somewhat opposed or strongly opposed?

Occupation	Pro: Strongly	Somewhat	Opposed
Owner small enterprise	48	45	7
Owner big enterprise	46	50	4
Blue-collar worker	45	47	7
Self-employed	42	53	5
Qualified civil servant	40	49	11
Agricultural worker	38	51	11
Qualified white collar	36	56	9
White collar	34	57	9
Qualified blue collar	32	60	9
Executive civil servant	30	58	12
Executive white collar	28	60	12
Civil servant	26	59	15

Sources: New Democracies Barometer 3, 1994; N = 5,705 employed persons (= Bulgaria, the Czech Republic, Hungary, Poland, Romania, Slovakia, Slovenia, the Ukraine combined).

The third rank in occupational groups who favour EU accession is blue-collar labour of unskilled and skilled workers. Within that occupational stratum, 45 per cent strongly support their country joining the European Union. This sympathy of labourers for European Integration might relate to the expectation of the blue-collar workers in many post-Communist countries to change labour markets and move to better working conditions in other EU member states after EU accession. The prospect of an enlarging Europe seems to be appealing to agricultural workers, too: 38 per cent of agricultural workers strongly support their country joining the European Union. One possible explanation for this high support by farm workers could be based upon the assumption that the system of agricultural subsidies as part of European agricultural policies of the European Commission is attractive for people involved in the agricultural sector in Central and South-East Europe.

Another professional group which strongly supports the process of EU enlargement is white-collar labour. The strongest support is expressed by 40 per cent of the qualified civil servants, followed by 36 per cent of qualified white-collar workers and by 34 per cent of normal white-collar workers. Somewhat lower is the strong support for the EU accession in the group of qualified blue-collar workers (32 per cent) and executive white-collar labour (28 per cent).

The assumption of a significant influence of the urban–rural dimension, one of the classical cleavages described by Seymour M. Lipset and Stein Rokkan (1967), upon attitudes towards EU accession is supported only to some extent by empirical evidence on the basis of our comparative

Table 8.14 Urban–rural divide and EU accession

	<5,000	*<20,000*	*<100,000*	*>100,000*	*Diff.*
Accession countries					
Slovakia	30	43	43	60	+30
Hungary	23	30	34	41	+18
Romania	30	51	38	41	+21
Slovenia	26	32	39	37	+13
Poland	30	*	34	35	+5
Other countries					
Croatia	55	53	57	53	+4
FR of Yugoslavia	36	44	44	44	+8
Belarus	21	30	25	32	+11
Russia	16	*	25	31	+15

Sources: New Democracies Barometer 5 (1998). Russian Federation Survey 1994; N = 3.535.

Note
Percentage strongly in favour of EU accession (Town size).

and cross-national research. The general support for EU membership is in many, but by far not all, cases positively associated with the size of a town, where the respondent lives (see Table 8.14). The core group of post-Communist citizens, who are 'strongly in favour' of their own country joining the European Union in the foreseeable future are those who live in big cities with more than 100,000 inhabitants. In cities like Prague, Budapest, Bratislava, Warsaw, etc., altogether 43 per cent are strongly in favour of EU enlargement, which is the highest share in comparison with other town sizes. In villages with less than 5,000 inhabitants, only 31 per cent support the EU accession of their own country. In Central Europe we find a linear association between town size and support for European integration, whereas in South-East Europe people in cities with less than 20,000 inhabitants are more oriented towards Europe than in cities between 20,000 and 100,000 inhabitants, which breaks the linear pattern.

In Slovakia the urban–rural divide is polarising Slovak society with regard to the EU accession of that country. In Slovak villages, only 30 per cent strongly favour the process of European integration; in middle cities of between 20,000 and 100,000 inhabitants we find a constant share of 43 per cent of Slovaks who support the integration of Slovakia into the European Union. The peak of EU support is finally reached in Slovak cities with more than 100,000 inhabitants: in these regional and national urban centres, an absolute majority of 60 per cent strongly favour the process of Slovakia joining the European Union.

The correlation between urbanisation and Europeanisation in terms of enlargement of the European Union is clear-cut in Hungary, too. One-fifth of Hungarians living in rural areas (23 per cent) is in favour of Hungary joining the European Union during the first round of enlargement. This share of pro-Europeans goes up to 34 per cent of Hungarians dwelling in cities of between 20,000 and 100,000 inhabitants, whereas the most supporters for EU accession can be found again in the biggest Hungarian cities with more than 100,000 inhabitants, where 41 per cent can be labelled strong supporters of the EU accession of Hungary. In Slovenia, one-quarter of Slovenes living in villages and small towns with less than 5,000 inhabitants are in favour of Slovenia joining the European Union. This share goes up to 32 per cent of Slovenes who live in small towns of between 5,000 and 20,000 inhabitants. In all other cities with more than 20,000 inhabitants, the share of pro-Europeans is rather constant around 38 per cent, and the share of EU supporters is even slightly lower in the capital Ljubljana than in other relatively big cities in Slovenia. In Poland, as in many other analyses of the impact of social structure upon EU accession, the influence of the urban–rural divide is visible, but rather limited. In Polish villages, 30 per cent support the future EU membership of Poland. That share goes up to 34 per cent in Polish towns of between 20,000 and 100,000 inhabitants and slightly more up to 35 per cent in big Polish cities with more than 100,000 inhabitants. We can therefore speak of a comparatively high homogeneity of Polish society along the urban–rural dimension with regard to EU enlargement.

The impact of the urban–rural divide is much less obvious in South-East Europe in comparison with the analogous patterns in Central Europe. In Romania, for example, we find the highest level of support for Romania joining the European Union in towns of between 5,000 and 20,000 inhabitants, where an absolute majority of 51 per cent strongly supports EU membership of their home country. EU support in Belarus is very volatile along the urban–rural dimension, oscillating between 20 and 30 per cent without any clear direction and link with the size of a specific Byelorussian town. In the Federal Republic of Yugoslavia the issue of EU accession is not distributed along the urban–rural divide at all: in villages of up to 5,000 inhabitants we find a share of 36 per cent of the Serbian villagers in favour of EU accession, whereas in all other Serbian towns and cities of between 5,000 and big regional or national centres of more than 100,000 inhabitants the share of EU supporters is constantly 44 per cent. It was impossible to quantify the impact of the urban–rural dimension upon EU accession in the Federal Republic of Yugoslavia. In Croatia, finally, we have a very high degree of territorial homogeneity concerning the question of an integration of Croatia within the European Union. The share of Croats supporting the EU accession of Croatia in the future is in all types of villages and towns around 55 per cent with oscillations within the sampling error of the Croatian survey. In precise analogy to Serbia-Montenegro, it was impossible to identify any influence of the urban–rural divide upon attitudes towards EU accession in Croatia.

One central result is that the overall image of the European Union is very positive, especially in Slovenia, the Czech Republic and Poland. A negative image of the European Union is only supported by less then 10 per cent of all Central Europeans. An overwhelming majority of the Central European general public express the wish to join the European Union in the first wave of enlargement of the EU towards the East, better to say towards the centre. Strong support for joining the EU is especially visible in Hungary, Slovakia and the Czech Republic. In many aspects of EU accession, we found a striking homogeneity between the opinions of the Czech and the Slovak population despite clear differences of opinions and behaviour at the elite level and the level of the political systems of both countries.

Gender also plays a role: Central European men are more in favour of joining the European Union than Central European women. Age is also an important factor: the core group of support for the enlargement of the European Union is the Central European youth. The younger the respondent, the higher the support for joining the European Union. There was a clear pattern regarding the influence of education: rising levels of education resulted in growing support for the European Union. Another result of our study was that money matters in attitudinal patterns about the European Union too: higher levels of household income correlate positively with increasing support for EU membership. The core group of EU accession in Central European economies are the new group of entrepreneurs and the self-employed: they have the highest levels of support for EU membership, whereas the working class displays considerable levels of scepticism about the European Union in general and EU membership in particular.

Finally, the core group of 'New Europeans' with very positive attitudinal patterns lives to a large extent in the main Central European cities like Prague, Budapest and Warsaw and other large cities of the Central European buffer zone, which display the newly created market economy in a fascinating combination with the rich culture of the past.

Enlargement of the European Union: attitudes in EU member states

In this third section of the chapter we present the opinion of the general public in the fifteen member states of the European Union in two comparative perspectives. First, we compare which accession countries are more welcome and which to a lesser extent, and, second, if the public climate towards specific accession countries has undergone some changes in the period between 1998 and 2000. The database for this section is not our own survey data but results from the EUROBAROMETER, which is organised and conducted by the European Commission in general and by the Directorate for Education and Culture in particular. The EUROBAROMETER measures twice a year – every spring and autumn – the public opinion in all fifteen member states on current affairs and political issues with great significance for European Union policies.

The attitudes within the European Union towards the enlargement of the Union to the South on the one hand and to the East on the other are rather clear-cut: the most popular accession countries are two islands in the Mediterranean sea, Malta and Cyprus (see Table 8.15). A majority of 50 per cent of all EU citizens are in favour of Malta joining the EU, a share which is constant during the observation period between October 1998 and May 2000. The strongest support for the accession of Malta is to be found in Greece (68 per cent in favour), Sweden (65 per cent), the Netherlands (63 per cent), Italy (60 per cent) and the United Kingdom (58 per cent). The support for Cyprus joining the EU with a share of 44 per cent of all EU citizens is quite high too. It is not surprising that 87 per cent of the Greek population are in favour of Cyprus joining the European Union as part of the next wave of enlargement. Also rather high is the wish in Sweden for Cyprus to join the EU (57 per cent), Denmark (51 per cent), Spain, Italy and Ireland with 50 per cent each supporting the integration of Malta and finally the United Kingdom, where 48 per cent of the British are in favour of including Malta as a new member state of the European Union. The most popular accession country from post-Communist Eastern Europe is Hungary: a stable majority of 46 per cent of all EU citizens between Dublin and Athens are in favour of Hungary joining the European Union. The case of Hungary is very interesting. The highest level of support for Hungarian membership is to be found in Scandinavia: 66 per cent of the Danish as well as the Swedish citizens are in favour of Hungary joining the EU, followed by Finland, where 64 per cent support the integration of Hungary. Also quite favourable is the pro-Hungarian climate in Greece (59 per cent in favour) and in the Netherlands (58 per cent). There is an absolute majority for Hungarian integration in Spain (52 per cent), and surprisingly in Austria,

Table 8.15 Support for EU enlargement within the Union, 1998–2000

	98/10 EB 50	99/5 EB 51	99/10 EB 52	00/5 EB 53	Diff. 50–53
Malta	52	50	50	50	−2
Hungary	50	46	46	46	−4
Cyprus	45	42	42	44	−1
Poland	47	43	43	44	−3
Czech Republic	45	40	40	41	−4
Slovakia	40	35	35	37	−3
Estonia	39	36	36	36	−3
Latvia	39	35	35	36	−3
Bulgaria	39	35	35	36	−3
Lithuania	38	35	35	35	−3
Slovenia	36	32	32	34	−2
Romania	37	33	33	34	−3

Source: European Commission, Eurobarometer Survey, DG Education and Culture.

Note
Percentage in favour of country becoming part of the EU.

too (52 per cent). If you consider a threshold of 40 per cent support within the EU for membership in the foreseeable future, only Poland and the Czech Republic are able to join Hungary in that top group of post-Communist countries as part of a potential first wave of enlargement in the new century. One might argue that Poland is more or less in the same position as Cyprus and Hungary: in spring 2000, a majority of 44 per cent of all EU citizens in the fifteen member states were clearly in favour of Poland becoming a full member of the EU. The countries most enthusiastic about Polish accession are Sweden (69 per cent in favour) and Denmark (67 per cent), followed by the Netherlands (62 per cent) and Greece (55 per cent). The acceptance of Poland being part of the next wave of enlargement is only slightly lower in Spain and Finland, where 52 per cent of the national populations are in favour of Poland joining the European Union. The support for full European integration of the Czech Republic decreased slightly from 45 per cent of all EU citizens in 1998 to 41 per cent of the fifteen general populations in May 2000. The case of the Czech Republic shows further evidence of the massive support of the Eastern enlargement of the EU within the Scandinavian countries: an absolute majority of 68 per cent of the Swedes, of 62 per cent of the Danes as well as 53 per cent of the Finnish population would like the Czech Republic to become a full member of the European Union. The two Southern countries, Greece (56 per cent) and Spain (50 per cent), are in favour of the integration of the Czech Republic as well.

The second group of Central and Eastern European accession countries in terms of their popularity within the current European Union consists of Slovakia, Estonia, Latvia and Bulgaria. The support of EU citizens for these four countries and their ambitions to join the European Union stabilised between 36 and 37 per cent in the spring of 2000. This intermediate level of support is more or less constant in 1999 and 2000 and represents only a small decrease compared to the generally higher levels of support for enlargement in 1998. The pattern of support for Slovakia is very similar to the pattern with regard to the Czech Republic: the core group of support comes from Scandinavia with a majority of 68 per cent in Sweden, 57 per cent in Denmark and finally 53 per cent in Finland in favour of Slovakia joining the European Union with the next wave. The pattern of support for Estonia and Latvia is exactly the same: approximately 70 per cent of all Danes, Finns and Swedes wish that both Baltic countries should become members of the European Union as part of the upcoming round of EU enlargement. Bulgaria is also supported by two Scandinavian countries, by Sweden (52 per cent in favour), on the one hand, and by Denmark (48 per cent), on the other. The crucial support for Bulgaria seems to derive from her neighbour Greece, where a majority of 57 per cent of the Greek population express their wish for Bulgarian integration.

The third group with the lowest levels of support from within the EU are Lithuania, Romania and, quite surprisingly, Slovenia. These three least

popular accession countries are backed by only between 34 and 35 per
cent of all EU citizens. The integration of Lithuania is backed – almost
exclusively – by 70 per cent of the Swedish and the Danish population as
well as by 56 per cent of the Finnish population. It appears to be quite surprising that only 34 per cent of the general population of all EU member
states are in favour of Slovenia joining the European Union. The driving
force for bringing Slovenia into the European Union are not her neighbours, but the Scandinavian cluster of Sweden (54 per cent in favour) and
Denmark (51 per cent). Support for Slovenian membership is rather high
in Greece (50 per cent), Spain (47 per cent), and to a lesser extent by her
neighbour Italy (40 per cent). The latter phenomenon might be caused
by several unsettled territorial issues and the issue of restitution. The integration of Romania finally gets some support by Greece (54 per cent in
favour), Spain (48 per cent) and Italy (44 per cent). In addition, the
Scandinavian countries, which could be described as the spearhead of
enlargement of the European Union, support the integration of Romania
too. A majority of about 50 per cent of the Danish and Swedish citizens
are in favour of Romanian integration.

The dimension of negative feelings against certain candidate countries
is covered on the basis of those citizens within the European Union, who
are against a certain accession country becoming a EU member as part of
the first wave of enlargement in the new century (see Table 8.16). The
most unpopular candidate countries are Romania, Slovenia and Bulgaria.
A relative majority of 42 per cent of the EU citizenry is against Romania
joining the European Union. These anti-Romanian feelings are highest in
Austria (69 per cent against), Germany (59 per cent against), Belgium

Table 8.16 Resistance to enlargement within the Union, 1998–2000

	98/10 EB 50	99/5 EB 51	99/10 EB 52	00/5 EB 53	*Diff.* 50–53
Romania	40	43	42	42	+2
Slovenia	38	42	41	40	+2
Bulgaria	36	40	39	39	+3
Estonia	36	38	38	38	+2
Latvia	36	38	38	38	+2
Lithuania	36	39	39	38	+2
Slovakia	36	39	38	38	+2
Czech Republic	31	35	35	35	+4
Poland	32	35	35	34	+2
Cyprus	36	33	33	32	−4
Hungary	28	31	31	31	+3
Malta	25	26	27	26	+1

Source: European Commission, Eurobarometer Survey, DG Education and Culture.

Note
Percentage EU respondents against a country becoming part of the EU.

and France. Quite strong is the opposition within the EU general populations against Slovenia: 40 per cent of respondents between Lisbon and Berlin dislike the idea of Slovenia becoming a member state of the European Union. The anti-Slovenian climate within the EU is most visible in France (52 per cent against), German (50 per cent against) and Belgium (50 per cent against). Number 3 in the negative list of enlargement is Bulgaria, where a stable relative majority of 39 per cent of all EU citizens is against EU membership during the next wave of enlargement. The climate against Bulgaria is not very favourable in Austria (65 per cent against), Germany and Belgium (both 51 per cent against) and in France (50 per cent against). The intermediate group of accession countries with a certain resistance from within the European Union are the three Baltic countries and Slovakia: there is a stable group of 38 per cent of the EU citizenry, which is against the integration of these four countries. The opposition against the three Baltic countries joining the European Union is quite strong in France (53 per cent) and Austria (50 per cent), but also well above the European average in Germany (44 per cent) and in Belgium (48 per cent). The citizens within Europe do not differentiate between Estonia, Latvia and Lithuania, the percentages are approximately the same for all three Baltic countries in the negative as well in the positive directions. The anti-Slovak attitudes are to be found – surprisingly – in Austria, which is its immediate neighbour (57 per cent against) and in France (52 per cent), but also rather explicit in Belgium (49 per cent) and in Germany (45 per cent).

Only one-third of the EU citizens are explicitly against the Czech Republic and Poland becoming a fully-fledged member of the European Union during the process of enlargement, the latter being, since the summit of Nice, the number one political issue on the European agenda. The anti-Polish sentiments are highest in Austria (60 per cent), followed by Germany and Belgium (both 46 per cent against) and France (45 per cent). The opposition within the EU against the integration of the Czech Republic shows a very similar picture: the Austrian population is quite hostile regarding the European integration of their Czech neighbour (49 per cent against); a comparable level of opposition against the Czech Republic can be found in France (48 per cent) and Belgium (47 per cent), followed by Germany (41 per cent). The opposition against Hungary, Malta and Cyprus becoming a full member of the EU is by far the smallest: only 32 per cent resent the integration of Cyprus, another 31 per cent are against Hungarian membership to the EU, and one-quarter of the EU citizenry expresses some doubts about the usefulness of Malta as a new member of the European Community. The opposition against Malta is strongest in France (46 per cent against), Austria (45 per cent), Germany (41 per cent) and Belgium (39 per cent). Surprisingly, we found only two countries with a significant opposition against Hungary joining the EU, France (47 per cent) and Belgium (44 per cent). The shrinking (or dwindling) opposition against Malta as a new EU member has its stronghold in France (42 per cent), Austria (35 per cent), Germany (34 per cent) and Belgium.

The aim of this chapter is to report attitudes towards enlargement in the fifteen member states of the European Union, seven candidate countries for enlargement, and five other post-Communist states not currently negotiating EU membership. This chapter finds more than one-fifth of all citizens in the accession countries regard themselves as Europeans. These post-Communist Europeans tend to be young, well educated and city dwellers. In the candidate states, an absolute majority of post-Communist citizens regard the activities of the EU as positive and more than 90 per cent favour the integration of their own country into the European Union. The core groups for joining are again the young, better off, highly educated and urban residents of candidate countries. Among the EU member states attitudes follow geographical clusters: the driving forces of opinion are the Scandinavian EU countries and Mediterranean countries, Greece, Spain and Italy. The strongest opposition to enlargement is found among citizens of Austria, Germany, Belgium and France. The favourite countries of EU citizens for enlargement are Malta, Cyprus and Hungary; the least popular candidate countries are Romania, Slovenia and Bulgaria.

European identity, enlargement and democracy

When all the elements of European identity and enlargement of the European Union, which have been analysed in this chapter, are brought together in a multivariate model, it turns out that European issues and European identity contribute only 2 per cent to the overall explained variance of support for democracy in post-Communist Europe. The most important variable for democratic support is if the post-Communist citizen displays a positive evaluation of the activities of the European Union (beta = 0.08) (see table 8.17).

The effect of a positive image of the European Union upon a basic democratic orientation grew from a regression coefficient of 0.03 in 1994 to 0.08 in 1998. The second most important 'European' influence regarding the democratisation of the general public in Central and Eastern Europe is support for membership of the own country in the European

Table 8.17 European integration and democracy

	1994	*1998*	*Change*
Positive image of EU	+0.03	+0.08	+0.05
Support for EU accession	+0.14	+0.06	−0.08
European identity	+0.09	+0.03	−0.06
R^2	0.03	0.02	−0.01
Significance	0.00	0.00	0.00

Union. The fact that somebody is very interested in their country joining the EU is highly correlated with being democratic. The third factor relates to European identity. The impact of being European upon being democratic decreased from a regression coefficient of 0.09 in 1994 to 0.03 in 1998. The spread of European identity in post-Communist Europe seems to go well beyond the core group of democrats in Central and Eastern Europe. Obviously, it is possible to adopt a European identity without being – automatically – a fully-fledged and developed democrat.

9 Conclusion

The analysis of political transformations in fifteen post-Communist countries for the period between 1991 and 1998 showed that we cannot and we should not speak of *one* post-Communist Eastern Europe, which would imply a homogeneity of the process of democratisation of the region, but of very different regions within the former 'Soviet bloc'. The book identified four different regions, which display diverging patterns of political change. The first and most advanced region is 'Central Europe', including Poland, the Czech Republic, Hungary, Slovenia and Slovakia. The second distinct region is 'Southern Europe', which encompasses Romania, Croatia, Bulgaria and the Federal Republic of Yugoslavia. The third post-Communist region, which crystallised in this book, is post-Communist 'Northern Europe', including Estonia, Lithuania and Latvia. Finally, the fourth post-Communist region is 'Eastern Europe', which includes Belarus, the Ukraine and the Russian Federation. The basic feature of these four regions is that we do not find a convergence of patterns of political development, but a clear divergence of paths of political change across these four main post-Communist regions.

The main innovation of this book consists in the conceptualisation and development of an 'index of democracy' (see Chapter 3), which for the first time enables comparative political science to measure with one single figure the extent and level of democratisation at the micro-level of political change, at the level of the post-Communist general public in fifteen countries. The micro-analysis of the complex processes of democratisation performed in this book showed that Poland, the Czech Republic and Hungary can already be labelled as 'consolidated democracies', because more than 60 per cent of the general public in these Central European countries are already 'democratic post-Communist citizens'. A clear-cut majority of the general public is also democratic in Slovenia and Slovakia, and Slovenia in particular is very close to the position of a consolidated democracy. The second level of democratisation is visible in post-Communist 'Southern Europe': Romania, Croatia and Bulgaria can be characterised as 'emerging democracies', because in all three Southern European countries more than 50 per cent of the population can be described as democrats, which is well beyond the threshold of 40 per cent Democrats for the type of emerging democracies. Serbia-Montenegro is a deviant case in Southern Europe, it is a transforming society with a uncertain outcome regarding the democratisation at the micro-level. In Northern Europe, only Estonia fulfils the criteria for an emerging democracy with a share of 46 per cent Democrats, whereas Lithuania and Latvia are transforming societies, where democracy is only one alternative amongst a variety of different types of political regimes. The lowest level of democratisation of the general public was identified in Eastern Europe. In the Ukraine and the Russian Federation, less than 20 per cent of the population are 'Democrats'. This low level of democratisation of the general public makes any future for democracy in Russia and the Ukraine very questionable and uncertain and leaves the way open for alternatives to democracy. A deviant and interesting case within Eastern Europe is Belarus, where the general public fulfils the criterion of an emerging democracy with a non-democratic macro-system ruling at the same time in Belarus. At the micro-level of the post-Communist citizen, Poland, the Czech Republic, Hungary, Slovenia, Slovakia, Romania, Croatia and Bulgaria are beyond the point of no return regarding the process of democratisation. Democracy as a form of political regime is more and more embedded in these eight societies during the process of political transformation. Estonia and Belarus are emerging democracies at the level of the population; here the interaction between micro-support for democracy and macro-actions of the political elites will decide the future course of democratisation in these countries. Democracy is in a very weak position in the Federal Republic of Yugoslavia, Lithuania, Latvia, the Ukraine and the Russian Federation with regard to the support by their own citizens. In these countries, the transformation to non-democratic regimes is not impossible and the outcome of political transformations, even ten years after the end of Communism, does not clearly indicate democracy. In these five transforming post-Communist societies, democracy appears to be only one option of political change, which is challenged by non-democratic alternatives.

Who are now the 'democrats' in post-Communist Europe? Is there a consistent social structure of support for democracy in post-Communism? The core group of democracy in all four post-Communist regions are citizens with tertiary education, living in major cities and the young generation. These social groupings are the avant-garde and stronghold of democracy at the micro-level of political transformation in all fifteen countries. In Central Europe, more than 80 per cent of all graduates are democrats, more than 70 per cent of people living in cities with more than 100,000 inhabitants show democratic attitudes and almost 70 per cent of the post-Communist Central European youth can be labelled as democratic. Hence, the recipe for future success of democracy in post-Communism appears to be modernisation in terms of better education and urbanisation of these societies, combined with a strong reliance on the democratising forces of the post-Communist youth between Prague and Moscow and their impact upon the post-Communist society as a whole.

After the development of the index of democracy, which is supposed to measure 'support for democracy' in post-Communist Europe, this phenomenon was used as a dependent variable. The main aim was to identify the core determinants for democratisation of the general population in post-Communist Europe. The main results of the analysis of the impact of a variety of dimensions upon support for democracy and of this book are displayed below:

1   Market economy (= Chapter 6)
    Macro-economic influences
    Explained variance: 27%
2   Household economy (= Chapter 5)
    Micro-economic influences
    Explained variance: 13%
3   Security and international conflict (= Chapter 7)
    International influences
    Explained variance: 7%
4   Social structure (= Chapter 4)
    Micro-social influences
    Explained variance: 4%
5   Enlargement and European identity (= Chapter 8)
    International influences
    Explained variance: 2%

First of all, these five spheres of influence together explain 53 per cent of the phenomenon 'support for democracy' at the level of the adult population in post-Communist Central and Eastern Europe. The foremost determinant of democratisation is located at the level of the macro-economic structures. The most important sphere of influence for democracy after the end of Communism consists in the successful creation and consolidation of a free market economy and its principles in a transforming economy. Only a successful market economy and the free development of its structures seem to be the necessary precondition for the successful process of democratisation. At least at the level of the general public and the individual post-Communist citizen we can postulate from that result that it appears to be impossible to have a sustainable democratisation without successful marketisation in a given transition society.

The second precondition after the existence of a well-accepted market economy seems to be the economic condition of the individual post-Communist household. These micro-economic influences on democratisation in post-Communist Europe account for 13 per cent of the explanatory power of these multivariate models of support for democracy in Central and Eastern Europe in the course of the third wave of democratisation. The positive impact on the democratic post-Communist citizen comes in this sphere from a general perception of being a micro-economic winner of transition. Less decisive in this respect is the exact balance sheet of the individual household at the end of the year, but the comparative improvement of the overall economic situation of the household with the Communist period. The macro-economic precondition of a working market economy and the micro-economic precondition of a winning post-Communist household together account for 40 per cent of the explanatory power of the core model of post-Communist democratisation. The other dimensions are more or less embellishment and detail compared to the dominance of economic preconditions of democracy in Central and Eastern Europe.

The sphere of international conflict and European security accounts for 7 per cent of the multivariate model of democratic transformation since 1989. Crucial variables associated with post-Communist democrats are the support for NATO membership on the one hand and the low feeling of threat from the United States of America on the other. The situation of a post-Communist citizen in a transforming society, dimensions like gender, age, religiosity or education, have a much smaller impact upon the process of democratisation at the level of the general public than economic spheres. These variables measuring the influence of social structure account for only 4 per cent of the explained variance, and significant associations with support for democracy have been found between education, age, town size and gender. The impact of European identity and European integration upon democratisation is rather marginal with an explained variance of 2 per cent. It appears to be the case that the emergence of a European identity in Central and Eastern Europe is linked to the process of democratisation of the post-Communist general populations, but not identical.

Appendix

NEW DEMOCRACIES BAROMETER (NDB)
Principal Investigator and Project Director: Christian Haerpfer
An International Academic Survey Programme to monitor
democratisation, marketisation and the development of civil society in
Post-Communist Europe

Country	1991	1992	1994	1996	1998
A. Central Europe	NDB 1	NDB 2	NDB 3	NDB 4	NDB 5
1. Czech Republic	660(1)	1.408(8)	1.167(18)	978(29)	1.017(39)
2. Hungary	1.019(2)	970(9)	1.060(19)	1.067(30)	1.017(40)
3. Poland	1.193(3)	1.113(10)	1.057(20)	1.057(31)	1.141(41)
4. Slovakia	291(4)	625(11)	574(21)	1.117(32)	1.011(42)
5. Slovenia	1.049(5)	1.013(12)	1.023(22)	1.000(33)	1.000(43)
B. Southern Europe					
6. Bulgaria	1.002(6)	1.164(13)	1.139(23)	1.184(34)	1.007(44)
7. Croatia	*	1.000(14)	1.000(24)	1.000(35)	1.000(45)
8. FRY	*	*	*	*	1.000(46)
9. Romania	1.000(7)	1.000(15)	1.000(25)	1.038(36)	1.241(47)
C. Eastern Europe					
10. Belarus	*	1.225(16)	2.067(26)	1.000(37)	1.000(48)
11. Russia	*	*	3.535(27)	*	*
12. Ukraine	*	1.000(17)	1.000(28)	1.000(38)	1.161(49)
Total N	6.214	10.518	14.622	10.441	11.595

Note
The numbers in cells are the number of face-to-face-interviews in a given country.

The New Democracies Barometer conducted in the period between 1991 and 1998 consisted of a total of 53.390 face-to-face interviews in 49 nation-wide and representative cross-sectional sample surveys in 12 post-Communist European countries. These 53,390 personal interviews form the main database for this book.

NDB 1 – New Democracies Barometer 1

Year: 1991

1. Czech Republic: 660 interviews
   Fieldwork by GfK – Prague
   Fieldwork co-ordinator: Professor Peter A. Ulram

2. Hungary: 1019 interviews
   Fieldwork by GfK – Budapest
   Fieldwork co-ordinator: Professor Peter A. Ulram

3. Poland: 1193 interviews
   Fieldwork by GfK – Polonia
   Fieldwork co-ordinator: Professor Peter A. Ulram

4. Slovakia: 291 interviews
   Fieldwork by GfK – Prague
   Fieldwork co-ordinator: Professor Peter A.Ulram

5. Slovenia: 1049 interviews
   Fieldwork by Department of Sociology, University of Ljubljana
   Fieldwork co-ordinator: Professor Niko Tos

6. Bulgaria: 1002 interviews
   Fieldwork by BBSS Sofia
   Fieldwork co-ordinator: Professor Andrej Raitschev

7. Romania: 1000 interviews
   Fieldwork by IRSOP
   Fieldwork co-ordinator: Dr.Petre Datculsecu

Total: 6214 interviews

NDB 2 – New Democracies Barometer 2

Year: 1992

1. Czech Republic: 1408 interviews
   Fieldwork by GfK – Prague
   Fieldwork co-ordinator: Professor Peter A. Ulram

2. Hungary: 970 interviews
    Fieldwork by GfK – Budapest
    Fieldwork co-ordinator: Professor Peter A. Ulram

3. Poland: 1113 interviews
    Fieldwork by GfK – Polonia
    Fieldwork co-ordinator: Professor Peter A. Ulram

4. Slovakia: 625 interviews
    Fieldwork by GfK – Prague
    Fieldwork co-ordinator: Professor Peter A.Ulram

5. Slovenia: 1013 interviews
    Fieldwork by Department of Sociology, University of Ljubljana
    Fieldwork co-ordinator: Professor Niko Tos

6. Bulgaria: 1164 interviews
    Fieldwork by BBSS Sofia
    Fieldwork co-ordinator: Professor Andrej Raitschev

7. Croatia: 1000
    Fieldwork by CEMA-MITROPA Zagreb
    Fieldwork co-ordinator: Dr. Karl Blecha
    The sample excluded war zones on Croatian territory.

8. Romania: 1000 interviews
    Fieldwork by IRSOP
    Fieldwork co-ordinator: Dr. Petre Datculsecu

9. Belarus: 1225 interviews
    Fieldwork by University of Minsk
    Fieldwork co-ordinator: Professor David Rotman

10. Ukraine: 1000 interviews
    Fieldwork by Ukrainian Academy of Sciences, Kiev
    Fieldwork co-ordinator: Professor Nikolai Churilov

Total: 10,518 interviews

NDB 3 – New Democracies Barometer 3

Year: 1994

1. Czech Republic: 1167 interviews
    Fieldwork by GfK – Prague
    Fieldwork co-ordinator: Professor Peter A. Ulram

2. Hungary: 1060 interviews
    Fieldwork by GfK – Hungaria
    Fieldwork co-ordinator: Professor Peter A. Ulram

3. Poland: 1057 interviews
   Fieldwork by GfK – Polonia
   Fieldwork co-ordinator: Professor Peter A. Ulram

4. Slovakia: 574 interviews
   Fieldwork by GfK – Prague
   Fieldwork co-ordinator: Professor Peter A.Ulram

5. Slovenia: 1023 interviews
   Fieldwork by Department of Sociology, University of Ljubljana
   Fieldwork co-ordinator: Professor Niko Tos

6. Bulgaria: 1139 interviews
   Fieldwork by BBSS Sofia
   Fieldwork co-ordinator: Professor Andrej Raitschev

7. Croatia: 1000
   Fieldwork by MITROPA Zagreb
   Fieldwork co-ordinator: Dr. Karl Blecha
   The sample excluded war zones and zones of occupation.

8. Romania: 1000 interviews
   Fieldwork by IRSOP
   Fieldwork co-ordinator: Dr. Petre Datculsecu

9. Belarus: 2067 interviews
   Fieldwork by Department of Sociology, University of Minsk
   Fieldwork co-ordinator: Professor David Rotman

10. Ukraine: 1000 interviews
    Fieldwork by SOCIS-GALLUP, Kiev
    Fieldwork co-ordinator: Professor Nikolai Churilov

11. Russian Federation: 3535 interviews
    Fieldwork by MNENIE Moscow
    Fieldwork co-ordinator: Dr. Grigorij A.Pashkov

Total: 14,622 interviews

NDB 4 – New Democracies Barometer 4

Year: 1996

1. Czech Republic: 978 interviews
   Fieldwork by GfK – Bohemia
   Fieldwork co-ordinator: Professor Peter A. Ulram

2. Hungary: 1067 interviews
   Fieldwork by GfK – Hungaria
   Fieldwork co-ordinator: Professor Peter A. Ulram

3. Poland: 1057 interviews
   Fieldwork by GfK – Polonia
   Fieldwork co-ordinator: Professor Peter A. Ulram

4. Slovakia: 1117 interviews
   Fieldwork by GfK – Bohemia
   Fieldwork co-ordinator: Professor Peter A.Ulram

5. Slovenia: 1000 interviews
   Fieldwork by Department of Sociology, University of Ljubljana
   Fieldwork co-ordinator: Professor Niko Tos

6. Bulgaria: 1184 interviews
   Fieldwork by BBSS Sofia
   Fieldwork co-ordinator: Professor Andrej Raitschev

7. Croatia: 1000
   Fieldwork by MITROPA Zagreb
   Fieldwork co-ordinator: Dr. Karl Blecha

8. Romania: 1000 interviews
   Fieldwork by GfK Romania
   Fieldwork co-ordinator: Professor Peter A.Ulram

9. Belarus: 1000 interviews
   Fieldwork by Department of Sociology, University of Minsk
   Fieldwork co-ordinator: Professor David Rotman

10. Ukraine: 1000 interviews
    Fieldwork by SOCIS-GALLUP, Kiev
    Fieldwork co-ordinator: Professor Nikolai Churilov

Total: 10,441 interviews

NDB 5 – New Democracies Barometer 5

Year: 1998

1. Czech Republic: 1017 interviews
   Fieldwork by GfK – Bohemia
   Fieldwork co-ordinator: Professor Peter A. Ulram

2. Hungary: 1017 interviews
   Fieldwork by GfK – Hungaria
   Fieldwork co-ordinator: Professor Peter A. Ulram

3. Poland: 1141 interviews
   Fieldwork by GfK – Polonia
   Fieldwork co-ordinator: Professor Peter A. Ulram

4. Slovakia: 1117 interviews
   Fieldwork by KMG Bratislava
   Fieldwork co-ordinator: Dr. Karl Blecha

5. Slovenia: 1000 interviews
   Fieldwork by PR+PM Maribor
   Fieldwork co-ordinator: Dr. Znuderl

6. Bulgaria: 1184 interviews
   Fieldwork by GfK Bulgaria
   Fieldwork co-ordinator: Professor Peter A.Ulram

7. Croatia: 1000
   Fieldwork by MITROPA Zagreb
   Fieldwork co-ordinator: Dr. Karl Blecha

8. Romania: 1000 interviews
   Fieldwork by CSOP Bucharest
   Fieldwork co-ordinator: Dr. Karl Blecha

9. Belarus: 1000 interviews
   Fieldwork by Department of Sociology, University of Minsk
   Fieldwork co-ordinator: Professor David Rotman

10. Ukraine: 1161 interviews
    Fieldwork by SOCIS-GALLUP, Kiev
    Fieldwork co-ordinator: Professor Nikolaj Churilov

11. Federal Republic of Yugoslavia
    Fieldwork by ARGUMENT, Belgrade
    Fieldwork co-ordinator: Dr. Zdenka Milisjevic
    The sample included the territories of Serbia and Montenegro.

Total: 11,595 interviews

Further information: haerpfer@ihs.ac.at

Bibliography

Agh, A. (1998) *The Politics of Central Europe*, London: Sage Publications.

Bayli, T.A. (1994) *Presidents vs. Prime Ministers: Executive Authority in Eastern Europe*, Glasgow: Centre for the Study of Public Policy. University of Strathclyde.

Beyme, K. von (1994) *Systemwechsel in Osteuropa*, Frankfurt: Suhrkamp.

Boeva, I. and Shironin, V. (1992) *Russians between State and Market: The Generations Compared*, Glasgow: Centre for the Study of Public Policy. University of Strathclyde.

Brubaker, R.W. (1996) *Nationalism Reframed: Nationhood and the National Question in the New Europe*, Cambridge: Cambridge University Press.

Bryant, C.G.A. and Mokrzycki, E. (1994) *The New Great Transformation? Change and Continuity in East-Central Europe*, London: Routledge.

Burnell, P. (1994) 'Preface: Democratization and Economic Change Worldwide: Can Societies Cope?', *Democratization*, 1, 1–7.

Cammack, P. (1994) 'Political Development Theory and the Dissemination of Democracy', *Democratization*, 1, 353–74.

Cowen-Karp, R. (1993) *Central and Eastern Europe: The Challenge of Transition*, Oxford: Oxford University Press.

Dalton, R.J. (1999) 'Political Support in Advanced Industrial Democracies', in Norris, P. (ed.) *Critical Citizens' Global Support for Democratic Government*, Oxford: Oxford University Press, pp. 57–77.

Dawisha, K. and Parrott, B. (1997) *The Consolidation of Democracy in East-Central Europe*, Cambridge: Cambridge University Press.

Diamond, L. (1994) 'Rethinking Civil Society: Toward Democratic Consolidation', *Journal of Democracy*, 5, 4–17.

Diamond, L. (1999) *Developing Democracy Toward Consolidation*, Baltimore: Johns Hopkins University Press.

Dix, R.H. (1994) 'History and Democracy Revisited', *Comparative Politics*, 27, 91–106.

Duch, R.M. (1993) 'Tolerating Economic Reform: Popular Support for Transition to a Free Market in the Former Soviet Union', *American Political Science Review*, 87, 590–608.

Eberwein, W.-D. (1992) *Transformation Processes in Eastern Europe: Perspectives from the Modelling Laboratory*, Frankfurt/Main: Peter Lang.

Eckstein, H. (1988) 'A Culturalist Theory of Political Change', *American Political Science Review*, 82, 789–804.

Elster, J., Offe, C., Preuss, U.K., Boenker, F., Goetting, U. and Rueb, F.W. (1998)

Institutional Design in Post-Communist Societies: Rebuilding the Ship at Sea, Cambridge: Cambridge University Press.

Finifter, A.W. and Mickiewicz, E. (1992) 'Redefining the Political System of the USSR: Mass Support for Political Change', *American Political Science Review*, 86, 857–74.

Fullerton, M., Sik, E. and Toth, J. (1995) *Refugees and Migrants: Hungary at the Crossroads*, Budapest: Hungarian Academy of Sciences.

Gellner, E. (1983) *Nations and Nationalism*, Ithaca, NY: Cornell University Press.

Gellner, E. (1994) *Encounters with Nationalism*, Oxford: Blackwell.

Gellner, E. (1996) 'Dominant Minorities', title of conference organized at Central European University, Nationalism Centre: Prague.

Gibson, J.L. (1993) 'Perceived Political Freedom in the Soviet Union', *Journal of Politics*, 55, 936–74.

Gibson, J.L. and Duch, R.M. (1993) 'Emerging Democratic Values in Soviet Political Culture', in Miller, A.H., Risinger, W.M. and Hesli, V.L. (eds) *Public Opinion and Regime Change: The New Politics of Post-Soviet Societies*, Boulder: Westview Press, pp. 69–94.

Giddens, A. (1993) *Sociology*, Cambridge: Polity Press.

Green, A.T. and Skalnik-Leff, C. (1997) 'The Quality of Democracy: Mass Elite Linkages in the Czech Republic', *Democratization*, 4, 63–87.

Haerpfer, C.W. (1993) 'Demokratie und Marktwirtsschaft in Osteuropa im Trend', in Plasser, F. and Ulram, P.A. (eds) *Transformation oder Stagnation? Aktuelle politische Trends in Osteuropa*, Vienna: Signum Verlag, pp. 113–31.

Haerpfer, C.W. (1998) 'New Democracies Barometer: Attitudes Towards EU Accession in the Czech Republic, Hungary, Poland, Slovakia and Slovenia', in Klima, M. and Mansfeldova, Z. (eds) *The Role of the Central European Parliaments in the Process of European Integration*, Prague: Czech Academy of Sciences, pp. 183–98.

Haerpfer, C. and Wallace, C. (1998) 'From Euphoria to Depression: Changing Attitudes Towards Market Reform and Political Reform in the Czech Republic in Comparative Perspective 1992–1998', Vienna: Institute for Advanced Studies Working Papers.

Haerpfer, C. and Wallace, C. (1999) 'Old and New Security Issues in Post-Communist Eastern Europe: Results of an 11 Nation-Study', *Europe-Asia Studies*, 51, 989–1011.

Hann, C. (1995) 'Intellectuals, Ethnic Groups and Nations: Two Late-Twentieth Century Cases', in Periwal, S. (ed.) *Notions of Nationalism*, Budapest: Central European University Press, pp. 106–28.

Helliwell, J.F. (1994) 'Empirical Linkages Between Democracy and Economic Growth', *British Journal of Political Science*, 24, 225–48.

Henderson, K. and Robinson, N. (1997) *Post-Communist Politics: An Introduction*, 1st edn. Hemel Hempstead: Prentice Hall.

Huntington, S.P. (1991) *The Third Wave: Democratization in the Late Twentieth Century*, Norman, OK: University of Oklahoma Press.

Inglehart, R. (1999) 'Postmodernization Erodes Respect for Authority, but Increases Support for Democracy', in Norris, P. (ed.) *Critical Citizens: Global Support for Democratic Government*, Oxford: Oxford University Press, pp. 236–56.

Inkeles, A. (1991) *On Measuring Democracy: Its Consequences and Concomitants*, New Brunswick, NJ: Transaction Publishers.

Klingemann, H.-D. (1999) 'Mapping Political Support in the 1990s: A Global

Analysis', in Norris, P. (ed.) *Critical Citizens: Global Support for Democratic Government*, Oxford: Oxford University Press, pp. 31–56.

Lewis, P.G. (1994) 'Democratization and Party Development in Eastern Europe', *Democratization*, 1, 391–405.

Linz, J.J. and Stepan, A. (1996) *Problems of Democratic Transition and Consolidation: Southern Europe, South America, and Post-Communist Europe*, Baltimore: Johns Hopkins University Press.

Lipset, S. and Rokkan, S. (1967) *Party Systems and Voter Alignments*, New York: Free Press.

McLean, I. (1994) 'Democratization and Economic Liberalization: Which is the Chicken and Which is the Egg?', *Democratization*, 1, 27–40.

Marples, D.R. (1999) *Belarus: A Denationalized Nation*, Amsterdam: Harwood Academic Publishers.

Merkel, W. (1998) 'The Consolidation of Post-Autocratic Democracies: A Multi-level Model', *Democratization*, 5, 33–67.

Mishler, W. and Rose, R. (1999) 'Five Years After the Fall: Trajectories of Support for Democracy in Post-Communist Europe', in Norris, P. (ed.) *Critical Citizens: Global Support for Democratic Government*, Oxford: Oxford University Press, pp. 78–99.

Moore, B. (1966) *Social Origins of Dictatorship and Democracy*, Boston: Beacon Press.

Norris, P. (ed.) (1999) *Critical Citizens: Global Support for Democratic Government*, Oxford: Oxford University Press.

Offe, C. (1994) *Der Tunnel am Ende des Lichts: Erkundungen der politischen Transformation im Neuen Osten*, Frankfurt: Campus Verlag.

Potter, D., Goldblatt, D., Kiloh, M. and Lewis, P. (1997) *Democratization*, Cambridge: Polity Press.

Rose, R. (1995) *New Baltics Barometer II: A Survey Study*, Glasgow: Centre for the Study of Public Policy.

Rose, R. (1996) *New Russia Barometer V: Between Two Elections*, Glasgow: Centre for the Study of Public Policy.

Rose, R. (1998) *Getting things done with social capital: New Russia Barometer VII*, Glasgow: Centre for the Study of Public Policy.

Rose, R., Boeva, I. and Shironin, V. (1993) *How Russians are Coping with Transition: New Russia Barometer II*, Glasgow: Centre for the Study of Public Policy.

Rose, R. and Haerpfer, C.W. (1992) *New Democracies between State and Market: A Baseline Report of Public Opinion*, Glasgow: Centre for the Study of Public Policy.

Rose, R. and Haerpfer, C.W. (1993) *New Democracies Barometer II: Adapting to Transformation in Eastern Europe*, Glasgow: Centre for the Study of Public Policy.

Rose, R. and Haerpfer, C.W. (1994a) *New Democracies Barometer III: Learning from What is Happening*, Glasgow: Centre for the Study of Public Policy.

Rose, R. and Haerpfer, C.W. (1994b) *New Russia Barometer III: The Results*, Glasgow: Centre for the Study of Public Policy.

Rose, R. and Haerpfer, C.W. (1994c) 'Mass Response to Transformation in Post-Communist Societies', *Europe-Asia Studies*, 46, 3–28.

Rose, R. and Haerpfer, C.W. (1995) 'Democracy and Enlarging the European Union Eastwards', *Journal of Common Market Studies*, 33, 427–50.

Rose, R. and Haerpfer, C.W. (1996) *New Democracies Barometer IV: A 10-Nation Survey*, Glasgow: Centre for the Study of Public Policy.

Rose, R. and Haerpfer, C.W. (1997) 'The Impact of a Ready-Made State', *German Politics*, 6, 100–21.

Rose, R. and Haerpfer, C.W. (1998a) *Trends in Democracies and Markets: New Democracies Barometer 1991–98*, Glasgow: Centre for the Study of Public Policy.

Rose, R. and Haerpfer, C.W. (1998b) *New Democracies Barometer V: A 12-Nation Survey*, Glasgow: Centre for the Study of Public Policy.

Rose, R. and Haerpfer, C.W. (1998c) 'Making Good Use of Multinational Surveys in Post-Communist Countries', in Walker, R. and Taylor, M.F. (eds) *Information Dissemination and Access in Russia and Eastern Europe*, Amsterdam: IOS Press, pp. 178–87.

Rose, R., Mishler, W.T. and Haerpfer, C.W. (1997) 'Social Capital in Civic and Stressful Societies', *Studies in Comparative International Development*, 32, 85–111.

Rose, R., Mishler, W.T. and Haerpfer, C.W. (1998) *Democracy and its Alternatives: Understanding Post-Communist Societies*, Oxford: Polity Press.

Rose, R., Vilmorus, Baltic Data House and Saar Poll (1997) *New Baltic Barometer III: A Survey Study*, Glasgow: Centre for the Study of Public Policy.

Rueschemeyer, D., Stephens, E. and Stephens, J. (1992) *Capitalist Development and Democracy*, Cambridge: Polity Press.

Schedler, A. (1998) 'How Should We Study Democratic Consolidation?', *Democratization*, 5, 1–19.

USIA (1997) *NATO Enlargement: Views from the European Continent*, Washington, DC: United States Information Agency.

Wallace, C. (1997) *Who is for Capitalism, Who is for Communism? Attitudes towards Economic Change in Post-Communist Eastern Europe: A 10-Nation Comparison*, Vienna: Institute for Advanced Studies.

Wallace, C. (1998) 'Crossing Borders: Mobility of Goods, Capital and People in the Central European Region', in Brah, A., Hickman, M. and Mac van Ghaill, M. (eds.) *Future Worlds: Migration and Globalisation*, London: Macmillans.

Wallace, C. (1999) 'Crossing Borders: Mobility of Goods, Capital and People in the Central European region', in Brah, A., Hickman, M. and Mac van Ghaill, M. (eds) *Global Futures: Migration, Environment and Globalisation*, pp. 185–209, London and New York: Macmillan.

Wallace, C., Chmouliar, O. and Sidorenko, E. (1996) 'The Eastern Frontier of Western Europe: Mobility in the Buffer Zone', *New Community*, 22, 259–86.

Wallace, C. Chmouliar, O. and Sidorenko, E. (1997) *The Central European Buffer Zone*, Vienna: Institute for Advanced Studies.

Wallace, C. and Haerpfer, C.W. (1998) 'Some Characteristics of the New Middle Class in Central and Eastern Europe: A 10-Nation Study', in Tilkidjiev, N. (ed.) *The Middle Class as a Precondition of a Sustainable Society*, Sofia: Association for Middle Class Development, pp. 158–68.

Wallace, C. and Shola, D. (2001) *Patterns of Migration in Central Europe*, Basingstoke and New York: Palgrave Publishers.

White, G. (1994) 'Civil Society, Democratization and Development (I): Clearing the Analytical Ground', *Democratization*, 1, 375–90.

White, S. (2000) *Public Opinion in Moldova*, Glasgow: Centre for the Study of Public Policy.

White, S., Batt, J. and Lewis, P.G. (1994) *Developments in East European Politics*, London: Macmillan Press.

White, S. and Rose, R. (2001) *Nationality and Public Opinion in Belarus and the Ukraine*, Glasgow: Centre for the Study of Public Policy.

White, S., Rose, R. and McAllister, I. (1997) *How Russia Votes*, Chatham, NJ: Chatham House Publishers.

Zuzowski, R. (1998) *Political Change in Eastern Europe Since 1989. Prospects for Liberal Democracy and a Market Economy*, London: Praeger.

Index